WILD
BERRIES
of Alberta

A FIELD GUIDE

Tom Cervenka

Publisher: Northern Bushcraft Publishing

Website: http://northernbushcraft.com

Book Design: Tom Cervenka

Editorial Support: Christine Murray

Reviewers: Neil Jennings, Dr. Matt Lavine, Tom Reaume, Nicole Cervenka, Scott Formaniuk, Colleen O'Neill, Paul Sissons

Photos: All photos in this book are reproduced with the generous permission of their copyright holders. See the photographic attributions section for a full list of interior credits and attribution codes.

Cover Photographs: Anne Elliott (main photo, bottom-b, bottom-c); Øyvind Tafjord (top-right-a); Jacob Enos (top-right-b) [CC-BY-2.0, deriv]; username geishaboy500 (top-right-c) [CC-BY-2.0, deriv] via flickr.com; Jason Hollinger bottom-a [CC BY 2.0, deriv] via flickr; Ted Garver (bottom-d).

Back Cover Photographs: Harry Guiremand top-left; Allan Carson top-center; Walter Siegmund top-right [CC-BY-2.5, deriv] via flickr.com; Matt Lavin bottom-left; Anne Elliott bottom-center; Piero Amorati borrom-right [CC BY 3.0, deriv].

Disclaimer: The information relating to the edibility of plants, as well as to the traditional techniques used to prepare and store them, is not based on personal experience and no judgement has been made on its validity.

Glossary: Terms are taken from WordNet 3.0 Copyright 2006 by Princeton University. All rights reserved. This database is provided "as is" and Princeton University makes no representations or warranties, express or implied. By way of example, but not limitation, Princeton University makes no representations or warranties of merchantability or fitness for any particular purpose or that the use of the licensed database will not infringe any third party patents, copyrights, trademarks.

Contents

CONTENTS

Acknowledgements

I would like to acknowledge the generosity of Anne Elliott, Dr. Matt Lavin, and the many other talented photographic contributors who made this guidebook possible. A complete list of contributors is provided in the back of the book. Special thanks to Linda Kershaw and George Dixon for their advice and for providing many of the hardest-to-find photos. I am deeply appreciative of the many Flickr and Wikimedia Commons users who made their work available under creative commons licensing. Such material helped me greatly in creating the web-based guides to wild edibles at northernbushcraft.com, which eventually developed into printed editions.

Thanks to Tom Reaume, Neil Jennings, Paul Sissons, Nicole Cervenka, and Scott Formaniuk for their valuable feedback in reviewing the material. I dedicate this book to Christine Murray, the girl with dragon eyes who never stopped supporting me.

Introduction

THIS guide is for anyone who wishes to identify Alberta's wild edible fruits and berries with confidence. It also provides an account of how Native American groups across North America prepared and preserved the berries that they collected. The text makes no assumption that the reader has a botanical background. The descriptions are more detailed than those of many floras but avoid technical botanical terminology.

Each species description includes full color photographs that capture the plant's form, fruit, flowers, and leaves. Backpackers, hikers, campers, and other nature enthusiasts will find the guide to be a highly detailed and lightweight addition to their kit. It covers not only berry-yielding plants, but more generally, plants that produce any edible berry-like fruit, including cherries, pomes, hips, cones and drupes. Edible leaves, roots, and other parts of the berry plants are also pointed out. Although the focus is on native species, also included are several non-native species are that have escaped cultivation and are likely to be encountered in the wild.

Roughfruit fairybells

CAUTION

The information presented within this book has been compiled from many sources and is presented for the reader's interest. The information relating to the edibility of plants, as well as to the traditional techniques used to prepare and store them, is not based on personal experience and no judgment has been made on its validity. In some cases, hazards exists regarding the fruits' edibility, including plant toxins, medical interactions, poisonous look-alikes and other plant defenses. This information is noted at the beginning of each species account.

Before using this guide, be sure to carefully read the introductory sections covering poisonous berries and plant identification.

ON BERRIES

In this book, the word "berry" is broadly used to refer to any berry-like fruit that encases seeds in an often tasty pulp. The pulp encourages animals to eat the berries, which helps to disperse the seeds. Non–berry-yielding plants might be at the mercy of the wind or insects to help spread their genetic material, but berry plants entice birds and other animals capable of dispersing the seeds over large distances.

The reddish color of many berries is one factor that helps to attract birds, which can see reds quite well, as opposed to insects, which cannot. In cases where animals other than birds eat the berries, there is still the benefit that once the seeds pass through the animals digestive system they will (unceremoniously) be deposited right back onto the ground, surrounded by natural fertilizer. In fact, some seeds are encased in material that must first pass through an animal's digestive system before germination can occur.

Since flowers develop into berries, the reader is invited to venture out well before berry season armed with the flower photographs that are provided for each species. These early reconnaissance missions are a strategic way locate the richest collection sites.

IDENTIFICATION

The correct identification of plants requires attention to detail. Those who rely solely on the photographs risk making a misidentification. All the relevant characteristics listed in the species description as well as those seen in the photographs should match the plant being scrutinized. It is best to err on the side of caution when uncertain of a plant's identity, and to never consume parts of an unknown plant. The inherent variability of plants can make even the seasoned naturalist uncertain at times. No two plants are the same and wild plants are even more variable than the cultivated varieties we are most familiar with, due to cross breeding. This genetic diversity makes them more challenging to identify.

Other factors that can complicate species identification are the effects of age and the environment on individual plants. A plant's form changes dramatically between the time it sprouts and the time it dies. Growing conditions, including the soil characteristics, rainfall, weather, sunlight, and the presence of other plants can affect not only size and robustness, but also a plant's coloration, overall form, flavor, and concentration of toxins.

POISONOUS BERRIES

Fortunately, there is no need to become overly concerned about accidentally consuming poisonous berries. The native berries that are sweet-tasting to humans are not generally poisonous. Among the more dangerous berries are the ornamental, non-native varieties that grow in gardens and in some cases have escaped cultivation and spread into surrounding woodland.

A piece of folk wisdom that periodically surfaces is the idea that wild edibles can be identified by taking note of the foods that animals such as squirrels and birds are eating. This is simply not true. The physiology of other animals, including their digestive systems, is different enough from our own that they can safely eat foods that are lethal to us. Some survival manuals describe an edibility test. The reader is instructed to eat only a small amount of an unknown food and then wait 8–12 hours before eating larger amounts. Although this approach is wiser than consuming unknown foods indiscriminately, adverse effects can still

occur. Even lethal plants can take 24 hours or longer to affect the body.

Berries and other plant parts do not necessarily fall into the neat categories of "edible" and "poisonous." Some species are categorized as both edible and/or poisonous depending on the source. There are a number of reasons for this apparent contradiction. One is that some berries have parts that are edible while other parts are poisonous (e.g., edible pulp with poisonous seeds or skin). Sometimes berries can only be safely eaten at certain stages of ripeness or when particular techniques have been used to reduce the concentration of toxins (e.g., drying, or cooking). In addition, berries that

Star-flowered false Solomon's seal (not poisonous)

are edible in small to moderate amounts can become toxic when eaten in excess or when consumed over a prolonged period of time.

Another factor to consider is contamination. Berries can become unsafe to eat when they become contaminated with pesticides, sewage, pollutants, or fungal infection. For this reason, any edibles that you collect should be washed before being consumed. The water used for washing should either come from a source that is known to be clean, or should be made safe for drinking by filtering, boiling, or using purifying tablets.

Bastard toadflax

Chokecherry

A person's own physiology and medical history is another factor that affects whether a plant or berry is edible. Some individuals are susceptible to particular toxins where others are not. The factors that can affect how a person will react to eating a plant or berry include age, allergies, pregnancy, and interactions with medication. In some cases, sufficient scientific research has not yet been carried out to determine the full nature and extent of a fruit's toxicity.

CONSERVATION

Berry picking is forbidden in national and provincial parks, but there are many other areas to find berries, including the river valleys and ravines of urban areas and in the countryside. Logged areas offer excellent berry-picking opportunities, since some of the tastiest berry-producing plants are colonizers of cleared areas.

Berry pickers can rest assured that collecting berries does not interfere with or damage the natural environment since berries are typically produced in excess of what can be collected recreationally or eaten by animals. However, foragers should follow good conservation habits and refrain from trampling vegetation, leaving litter, or damaging plants in the process of their activity. Berry picking tends to increase a person's appreciation for nature, and that appreciation may ultimately be the most important ingredient in any conservation strategy.

USING THE GUIDE

The species accounts within this guide are arranged with one species per page. The species have been sorted into three categories of berry color (red, blue, other). Within each color category, they are sorted by size, beginning with low, creeping herbs, then shrubs and finally trees. In some cases, similar-looking berries have been grouped together, irrespective of the size of the plant. For example berries that have a raspberry-like appearance have been grouped together, as have juniper berries and currants. Each species account includes:

A. scientific and common names
B. color photographs
C. bullet-point summary
D. warnings regarding hazards
E. eating & traditional use.
F. description of the species.
G. habitat and distribution in Alberta.

A. Scientific and Common Names

The scientific name for each species is provided at the top of the page, immediately above the photographs. The common names are listed at the beginning of each species account, with the preferred common name used as the header. Preferred common names are chosen on the basis of their frequency of occurrence across botanical and non-scientific literature. In some cases, the common name is instead cited from the USDA Plants Database in order to avoid using the same name for different species or to achieve a more uniform naming convention across related species. Listed after the preferred common name is a comma-separated list of alternate common names, with a forward slash (/) used to indicate interchangeability.

B. Color Photographs

Color photographs are provided as a part of each species account. The photos were selected for their ability to convey not only the appearance flower and fruit, but also the overall form of the plant, the shape of the leaves, and other identifying characteristics.

C. Bullet Point Summary

Each species account begins with bullet points that summarize the palatability of the berry, its size, and the size of the plant. In cases where the plant has edible parts aside from the fruit, such as roots or leaves, these are also listed. The summary is not a substitute for the full text of the species description, and is intended only to allow the reader to rapidly identify pages of interest.

D. Warnings Regarding Hazards

Prominent warnings at the beginning of the species accounts have been included where applicable and provide information relating to fruit toxicity, plant defenses, or other hazards associated with collection or consumption. The warnings often highlight particular demographics that are at risk when consuming particular toxins present in the fruit (e.g., children, pregnant or breast-feeding women, medical patients, and those with sensitive skin or other allergies). The warnings may also relate to over-consumption or extended use of the food.

E. Eating & Traditional Use

This section describes how the fruits and other edible parts of the plant are commonly used for food, both recreationally and commercially. It also provides an account of how Native North American groups and early settlers prepared and preserved the fruit, including those outside of Alberta. It should be noted that foods eaten by early peoples may not be considered palatable by modern standards. We have become accustomed to a diet much higher in carbohydrates, sugars, and other refined ingredients. Some of the less pleasant fruits may require time to be appreciated as an acquired taste. Others may have been eaten in the past but never favored or only eaten during times of starvation.

In some cases, special preparation made the fruits more palatable, such as cooking, drying, making into jams and jellies, or mixing with other fruits. Where berries and other plant parts are described as edible when raw the reader may also assume that they are edible when cooked or dried.

F. Description of the Species

Each species description begins with an overview of the form of the plant, followed by a detailed account of the major parts, including the stem, bark, branches, twigs, leaves, flowers, and fruits.

The use of botanical terminology is kept to a minimum to increase readability. Where unavoidable or necessary for clarity, botanical terms have been explained in-line and referenced in brackets. It is assumed that the reader will not necessarily have access to a ruler or other measuring device when in the field. For that reason, the dimensions of all plant parts are provided both in metric units and be reference to commonly understood measurements, such as shin-height, thumb-width, or palm-length. Although the size of shins, thumbs, and palms differ from one individual to another, the same can be said of plant parts, and the margins of error are comparable. Of course, the reader is free to rely strictly on the metric measurements.

The level of detail provided in each species account is generally equal to or greater than what is provided in a typical botanical reference book (flora). However, some plant characteristics that are of little interest to berry pickers have been omitted, such as details regarding the roots, rhizomes, or winter buds. It is assumed that the reader will be using the guide primarily in the spring, summer, and fall, when the leaves and either the flowers or fruits are present.

The leaf description begins with the leaf outline and the shape of the lobes and leaflets. It then covers leaf attributes including but not restricted to thickness, hairiness, serration, glandular dotting, and texture. It ends with an account of the leaf stalk, leaf arrangement, and fall colors.

The flower description begins with the flowering time and then discusses clustering, flower color, and overall dimensions. The petals, sepals, and stamens are described for every species where they are present, and if salient or noteworthy, the bracts, pistils, tendrils, thorns and other structures are also described in detail. In cases where male and female flowers occur on separate plants, both the male and female flowers are described to assist the reader in determining whether a particular plant can be expected to yield fruits.

The fruit description begins with the season that the fruit reaches maturity and describes the color, texture, size, shape, juiciness and taste. In many cases the text provides a description of the unripe fruit and information regarding the seeds, skin, and surface characteristics such as glandular dotting, hairiness, bloom, and opacity. It is also noted when the mature fruit persists on the plant, making it a candidate for winter foraging.

G. Habitat & Distribution in Alberta

Alberta has a diversity of habitats ranging from mountains and foothills to prairie grasslands and arctic tundra. These are associated with eco-regions which are delineated by elevation and several other factors including soil type, climate, and other vegetation.

In Alberta, the montane zone exists from 825–1520 m above sea level, and is dominated by coniferous forests that occur in mountain passes. The subalpine zone is between 1520 and 2135 m, and is characterized by the presence of Engelmann spruce. The alpine zone begins at 2135 m (lower in the northern Rockies) and is marked by the disappearance of continuous forest and the emergence of meadows and intermittent islands of dwarf vegetation. The eco-region of a geographical area is predictor of whether a species is likely to occur in that area.

The habitat section of each species account outlines the regions of Alberta where the species is known to occur in the wild and the types of habitats where it is likely to be encountered. The section typically begins by indicating whether the species is native to Alberta or was introduced. Some species were originally brought over from Europe or other parts of the world, either by accident or to be cultivated, and subsequently became naturalized.

The eco-regions are then referenced. For most native species, the elevation range is specified in terms of one or more general vegetation zones, including montane, subalpine, and alpine zones. Readers unfamiliar with the eco-region zones in Alberta will welcome the presentation of each species' distribution in terms of the major urban centers and quadrants of the province. The distribution information reflects the probability of finding a species at a particular location rather than an absolute indicator. The section ends by providing a listing of favored terrain and growing conditions for the species.

American black currant

🦋 The Berries 🦋

Common Bearberry

syn. Kinnikinnick, Pinemat Manzanita

- ▶ berries are dry, mealy and tasteless.
- ▶ berry is under 1 cm wide.
- ▶ shrub is ankle-high.

WARNING: The berries should not be eaten by children or women who are pregnant or breast-feeding. They may cause nausea or constipation and extended use may result in stomach or liver problems.

EATING: The raw berry is dry and mealy, but becomes sweeter with cooking and is a good source of carbohydrates. The berries can be eaten fresh, dried for storage, or used in jellies, jams, soups or strews. Whole berries can also reportedly be popped like popcorn. Bearberries were traditionally a staple food for a number of Native American peoples, who often stored them in oil or mashed them with fat before cooking them to counteract the dryness and to prevent constipation. Dried, ground-up berries were sometimes made into pemmican by mixing them into equal parts of melted fat and dried, ground-up buffalo meat. The Okanogan-Colville cooked the berries with venison or salmon and then dried them into cakes which were eaten with salmon eggs. The leaves were commonly dried and mixed with other smoking material. This mixture, or "Kinnikinnick" was smoked alone or added to tobacco.

DESCRIPTION: This creeping, evergreen shrub grows ankle-high (15 cm) and forms thick mats that can be over a meter wide. The flexible, woody stems are up to 1 m long and are covered with a thin, brownish red bark that becomes rough and peels with age. The stems branch frequently and often take root.

The dark green, leathery **LEAVES** are spatula-shaped, tapering at the base and rounded at the end. The leaf blade is rarely more than an inch long (1–2.5 cm), is just over half as wide, and has smooth surfaces and edges. The upper surface has impressed veins; the paler underside has veins forming a coarse network. The leaves have short (2–5 mm) stalks and are alternately arranged, but appear opposite when crowded on the stem.

In the spring and summer, nodding, urn-shaped **FLOWERS** emerge in clusters (racemes) of 3–10 at the branch tips. Each flower is white, under 1 cm long, and consists of five lobes that are fused into an urn-shape. The urn is constricted and pink at the neck, smooth on the outside and hairy on the inside. Within are eight or ten stubby, antenna-like stamens capped with large, reddish brown anthers. In the late summer, the flowers develop into smooth, red **BERRIES** (actually drupes) that resemble tiny apples. Each berry is a slightly flattened sphere no more than 1 cm in diameter. It contains a dryish, pale yellow pulp with five small (3–4 mm), crescent-shaped nutlets that are united in a central ball. The berries persist on the branch into the winter.

HABITAT: This common native plant grows from coastal to lower alpine elevations. In Alberta, it occurs at longitudes west of Edmonton and latitudes north of Edmonton. It can be found in dry, open woods and meadows, exposed rocky sites and sandy or gravelly slopes.

Red Fruit Bearberry

- ▶ berries are juicy but poor tasting.
- ▶ berry is under 1 cm wide.
- ▶ shrub is boot-high.

WARNING: The berries should not be eaten by children or women who are pregnant or breast-feeding. They may cause nausea or constipation. Extended use may result in stomach/liver problems.

EATING: The berries are edible but have a poor taste. They were occasionally collected by the Gwich'n people of Alaska, though they were not a favored food. They were sometimes eaten raw as a cold remedy and were also made into jam. The Inuit would place the berries into barrels along with salmonberries and use them as a winter food. Their water content and thick skin makes them difficult to dry.

DESCRIPTION: The plant is a creeping, deciduous shrub that grows past boot-height (15 cm) and often forms a vegetative mat. The woody stems have brown bark that can become shredded with age. The stems divide into short, smooth branches and twigs that are erect to creeping.

The **LEAVES** are spatula-shaped, narrowly tapering at the base and rounded at the end. The leaf blade is characteristically paper-thin and finely toothed, rarely exceeding half a finger (2–4 cm) in length. Net-like veins are visible on both sides of the leaf blade, and appear impressed on the upper surface, which is hairless. The underside is also hairless and is a paler shade of green. The leaves are alternately arranged on the twigs and have leafstalks that are "winged," meaning that the leaf blade extends down the sides of the stalk. The leaves turn deep red in the fall and persist on the shrub after they wither and die, dropping in the winter.

In the spring or early summer, urn-shaped **FLOWERS** appear in clusters (racemes) of 2–6 at the tips of branches, usually before the leaves unroll. The flowers are initially yellowish green, becoming creamy white. Each flower is about ½ cm long and has five lobes that are fused into the shape of an urn with a constricted neck. Within are ten short, antenna-like stamens that do not protrude. In the autumn, the flowers develop into juicy but poor-tasting **BERRIES** (actually drupes) that range from brick red to scarlet and have a strong skin. The berry is spherical, no more than 1 cm in diameter, and contains 4–5 hard seeds.

HABITAT: This native plant grows from lowland to alpine elevations. In Alberta it occurs throughout the Rocky Mountains and at latitudes north of Ft. McMurray. At higher elevations, it can be found in moist, mossy or rocky areas around mountain summits and in shrublands. At lower elevations if occurs in coniferous woodland, tundra, and moist, peaty soils, including along the edges of rivers, lakes and bogs.

Lingonberry

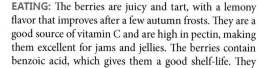

syn. Lowbush Cranberry, Cowberry

▶ berries are juicy and acidic.

▶ berry is up to 1 cm across.

▶ creeping shrub is ankle-high.

EATING: The berries are juicy and tart, with a lemony flavor that improves after a few autumn frosts. They are a good source of vitamin C and are high in pectin, making them excellent for jams and jellies. The berries contain benzoic acid, which gives them a good shelf-life. They are favored by recreational pickers and also used commercially in making pies, baked goods, candy, sauces, syrups and beverages. This berry has been an important food for northern peoples for centuries. Native Americans sometimes used the berries as an ingredient in pemmican. Above the Arctic Circle, the berries were traditionally eaten raw, cooked, or whipped with fat to make a sauce. The Gwich'in people mixed the berries with pounded, dried fish to make a dessert. The dried whole berries would be greased and placed in underground birchbark caches for storage. The leaves can be used in moderation to make a tea. They contain arbutin, which is used by pharmaceutical industry to treat intestinal disorders.

DESCRIPTION: This creeping evergreen shrub does not usually rise above ankle level (10 cm) though it can reach twice that height. It grows in dense colonies, forming mats of vegetation. The slender, semi-woody stems have splotchy brown bark and are no more than a couple millimeters thick. They either stand erect or creep along the ground for up to a foot (30 cm), forming roots. The many branches and young twigs are yellowish brown and minutely hairy, darkening with age.

The glossy, leathery **LEAVES** are narrowly elliptical to upside-down egg-shaped and have a rounded end that may be shallowly notched. The leaf blade is typically no longer than finger width (15 mm), is about a third as wide, and has smooth, downturned edges. The upper surface is shiny with only the midvein prominently recessed. The paler underside is brown-dotted. The leaves have virtually no stalks and are alternately arranged in a spiral.

In the late spring or early summer, nodding **FLOWERS** ranging from white to pinkish appear singly or in compact clusters (racemes) of 4–15 at the ends of branches. Each flower has four petals fused into a flaring cup or bell that is under 1 cm long. Within the bell is a white, protruding, rod-like pistil and eight antenna-like stamens capped with reddish purple anthers. By the late summer or autumn, the flowers have developed into shiny, red **BERRIES** that have an acidic taste. Each berry is spherical, up to 1 cm long and has a juicy flesh that contains 3–20 small (1 mm) yellowish seeds. The berries persist on the shrub into the winter.

HABITAT: This plant grows from lowland to alpine elevations. It is found in the western half of the province and at latitudes north of Edmonton. It occurs in coniferous forests and dry areas of peat bogs, often growing from decaying wood or old tree stumps. It can also be found on exposed sites, rocky barrens, and tundra.

Small Cranberry

syn. Northern/Bog Cranberry

▶ berries are juicy and very tart.

▶ berry is about 1 cm across.

▶ creeping shrub reaches ankle height.

EATING: The raw berry is juicy and has a sharp, sour flavor but it is one of the tastier cranberries and improves in flavor after freezing or cooking. It is high in pectin, which makes it good for jams and jellies or for mixing with other berries that are low in pectin. Because they are relatively difficult to gather in large quantities, they are not cultivated commercially in North America, though they are in Russia. Some Native American groups stored the berries in baskets and waited until they turned soft and brown to use them. The berries (raw or cooked) were also fire- or sun-dried and sometimes mixed with grease or oil before being and stored for winter. The Iroquois mashed them into small cakes, which were dried and later reconstituted in warm water for cooking into a sauce or eating with corn bread. The leaves can also be used to make a tea.

DESCRIPTION: The plant is a creeping evergreen shrub that grows to ankle height (10 cm), often forming dense vegetative mats. The slender, wiry stems have a thin, golden- to gray-brown bark that may exhibit fine splits or cracks. The stems are no more than 1 mm thick and up to half a meter long. They grow in a vinelike fashion along the ground, forming roots from where the leaves and branches attach. The branches and twigs are golden brown, flexible, and leafy.

The thick, leathery **LEAVES** are narrowly elliptical, tapering at both ends and ending with a pointed tip. The leaf blade is less than 1 cm long and has smooth edges that are rolled under. The upper surface is shiny and deep green and the underside is nearly white. The leaves have virtually no leaf stalks are alternately arranged.

In the early to midsummer, dark pink, nodding **FLOWERS** come into bloom. The flowers appear either singly or in clusters of several at the ends of stems. The flower is about 1 cm long and has four petals that curve strongly backwards. The petals surround eight antenna-like stamens that usually unite to form a long, pointed cone. The flower stalks are a few centimeters long and in the lower section, two tiny (1–2 mm) scale-like red bracts emerge. The flowers develop into **CRANBERRIES** that are initially white, turning pale pink and finally deep red when mature in the early fall. Each cranberry is spherical, about 1 cm wide and has a juicy, tart flesh that contains many seeds. The cranberries persist on the plant through the winter.

HABITAT: This common native plant grows from lowland to montane elevations. In Alberta it occurs in the western half of the province and at latitudes north of Edmonton. It can be found in alpine or arctic tundra and in the sandy or peaty soil in and around bogs, preferring the full sun.

Grouse Whortleberry

syn. Grouseberry

- berries are sweetly tart.
- berry is about half a centimeter wide.
- shrub reaches the lower shin.

EATING: The raw berries are juicy and tart with a pleasant flavor that only improves after cooking or freezing. They are suitable for use in jams, jellies, wine, pies, and other baked goods. Due to their small size and relatively low number, however, they are difficult to collect in quantity and are often left for the birds and other animals—the common name refers to the fact that grouse eat all parts of the plant. A number of Native American peoples, including the Kootenay, Okanagan and Shuswap used wooden or fish-bone combs to harvest the berries, which were eaten raw or sun-dried like raisins. The Cheyenne used the berries to treat nausea or increase appetite. The berries were sometimes fire-dried for storage and reconstituted in warm water. When dry, they were used as a flavoring agent or soup thickener. The boiled berries were be mixed with grease or oil for storage. A tea can be made from the fresh or dried leaves.

DESCRIPTION: The pant is a deciduous, broom-like shrub that usually does not grow past the lower shin (20 cm) and often forms extensive and dense colonies of clumpy, matted vegetation. The smooth, brownish stems are erect and closely branched, with many branches arise from the base of the stem, and forming roots where they meet moist ground. The branches are slender, light green to yellowish green, and have twigs that are strongly angled rather than being round.

The small, light green **LEAVES** are narrowly elliptical to egg-shaped, rounded or tapered at the base, ending with a pointed tip. The thin leaf blade is no longer than pinky finger width (7–11 mm) and up to half as wide, with edges that are finely toothed. The upper surface is light green and hairless. The underside is a duller, more pale green, net-veiny, and hairless. The leaves have virtually no leafstalks are alternately arranged on the branch.

In mid to late spring, solitary, pinkish, **FLOWERS** come into bloom, nodding on short stalks from were the leaves attach, usually on the lowest leaves of young shoots. The flowers are urn-shaped to bell-shaped and about ½ cm long. Within the urn are eight or ten tiny, hairless, antenna-like stamens. In the midsummer, the flowers develop into tiny, soft, **BERRIES** that range from bright red to wine-colored and taste sweetly tart. The berries are spherical and about ½ cm wide, remaining on the stem throughout the year.

HABITAT: This common plant is native to western North America and grows from foothill to subalpine elevations. In Alberta it occurs throughout the Rocky Mountains. It can found in dry to moist coniferous forests forming dense ground cover, as well in forest clearings, meadows, and on the sloping mass of loose rocks that are often found at the base of mountain cliffs.

Alpine Spicy Wintergreen

syn. Alpine Wintergreen

- ▶ berries are crisp and sour.
- ▶ berry is pea-sized.
- ▶ young leaves are edible raw.
- ▶ shrub grows below ankle height.

WARNING: The wintergreen flavor of the berries is caused by methyl salicylate, which can be toxic if consumed in excessive quantities. The plant should not be consumed or handled by children who are allergic to aspirin.

EATING: The leaves and berry-like fruits and leaves have a pleasant smell and a wintergreen flavor. The fruits are crisp and reminiscent of sour apples. They are used in preserves and are suitable for making jams, wines, sauces, and pies. The leaves, especially when young, are pleasant to eat as a trailside nibble, can be used as a potherb, or dried to make a tea.

DESCRIPTION: The plant is a creeping, evergreen shrub growing below ankle height (3–10 cm), forming a flat vegetative mat that is typically less than a foot (30 cm) across. The horizontal to leaning stems are closely branched and often red-hairy.

The leathery **LEAF** is broadly egg-shaped with a rounded base, ending with a rounded or bluntly pointed tip. The leaf blade is about an inch (2.5 cm) long and has thickened edges that are smooth or minutely toothed around the base. Both the upper and lower surfaces are smooth.

In the early to midsummer, solitary, white **FLOWERS** ranging from white to pinkish come into bloom, emerging from where the leaves attach. The flower is no more than ½ cm wide and has five petals. The petals are fused below the middle and form a hairless, cup-shaped bell. Within are ten antenna-like stamens capped with golden anthers. Immediately below and hugging the petals are five triangular, red sepals. The flower has a hairless, green stalk that bears a pair of tiny green, leaf-like bractlets that have reddish edges. By the fall, the flowers have developed into fleshy, dull red **BERRIES** (actually fruit capsules). Each berry is generally spherical, pea-sized (5–7 mm), and has a spicy taste.

HABITAT: This plant is native to western North America and grows from subalpine to alpine elevations. In Alberta, it occurs in the northern range of the Rocky Mountains. It can be found in moist mountain forests, mossy banks and rocky mountain slopes.

Wild Strawberry

syn. Scarlet/Virginia Strawberry

▶ berries are sweet, delicious.
▶ berry is about 1 cm across.
▶ plant reaches boot height.

EATING: The berries are sweet and delicious, with more flavor than the store-bought variety. They freeze well and can be cooked or made into jams, jellies and preserves. All parts of the plant are high in vitamin C. The berries were traditionally collected by many Native American groups, who ate them fresh or mashed them into small cakes that were dried for winter use. The unwilted leaves can be used to make a tea. Wilted leaves can contain toxins, and should not be consumed. The flowers, stems, and leaves can all be used for flavoring.

DESCRIPTION: This perennial herb rarely exceeds boot height (15 cm) and often grows in extensive colonies. It has several dull red, horizontal runners (stolons) that are a couple millimeters thick and over half a meter long. The runners are hairy, leafless, and form roots which grow into new plantlets. The leaf stalks and leafless flowering shoots both grow directly from the base of the plant. They are green to reddish and hairy.

The **LEAVES** are 3-parted, like a clover leaf, consisting of three short-stalked leaflets. Each leaflet is an inverted egg-shape, narrowing at the base, widest above the center and rounded at the end. The thin leaflet blade is rarely longer than a pinky finger (6 cm) and is about half as wide. The edges are coarsely toothed from the middle to the tip, with the end tooth characteristically narrower and shorter than its neighbors. The upper surface is smooth, bluish green and has a midvein that is prominently impressed. The underside is paler and silky-hairy.

In the late spring and early summer, white, scentless **FLOWERS** emerge singly or in open clusters (umbellate cymes) of 2–10 at the ends of shoots. The flowers are characteristically not as high as the surrounding leaves. Each flower is no more than inch-wide (2.5 cm) and has five round petals. The petals surround a yellow center that has 20–25 short, antenna-like stamens capped with yellow anthers. Just below the petals are five green, pointed sepals and five green, pointed bracts. In the summer, the flowers develop into red **STRAWBERRIES**. Each strawberry is roughly spherical, about 1 cm wide, and has sweet flesh with numerous small, yellow seeds (achenes) that are characteristically embedded in shallow pits on the surface.

HABITAT: This native plant grows in sunny location throughout Alberta, from lowland to subalpine elevations. It can be found in open woods, forest clearing and edges, and grassy areas. It also occurs by stream banks, lake shores, and in disturbed sites.

Woodland Strawberry

syn. Alpine Strawberry,
Wood/European Strawberry

- ▶ berries are sweet, strongly flavored.
- ▶ berry is about 1 cm across.
- ▶ plant grows to lower shin height.

EATING: These sweet strawberries have a delicious flavor and pleasant aroma. Because they are difficult to find and are quite small, they were usually eaten as a fresh delicacy by Native Americans. If plentiful, they were mashed, sometimes with Saskatoon berries, and spread out into cakes to dry in the sun. Every part of the plant is high in vitamin C. The unwilted leaves can be used fresh or dried for making a tea. Wilted leaves can contain toxins and should not be consumed.

DESCRIPTION: This deciduous perennial grows to the lower shin (25 cm), often forming large colonies. Its slender, trailing runners (stolons) are green to reddish and lightly or densely hairy. The runners have no leaves and form roots that become new plantlets.

The **LEAVES** have slightly hairy stalks and grow directly from the base of the plant. The leaf is compound, consisting of three stalkless leaflets arranged similar to a clover leaf. Each leaflet is an inverted egg-shape or elliptical, tapering at the base, widest above the middle and rounded or slightly pointed at the end. The blade of each leaflet is up to half a finger long (4 cm), about ⅔ as wide, and is sharply toothed along the edges of the upper half. The middle tooth at the end of the leaflet is characteristically longer than its neighbors. The upper surface of the leaflet is yellowish green and has straight veins that are prominently impressed. The paler underside is slightly hairy.

Starting in the late spring, white **FLOWERS** emerge in small, loose clusters of 2–10 on erect, downy stems that are characteristically higher than the leaves. Each flower is about thumb-wide (2 cm) and has five round to egg-shaped petals. The petals surround a yellow center of 20 short, antenna-like stamens. Just below the petals are five pointed, green sepals. In the summer, some of the flowers develop into **STRAWBERRIES** that are initially green and scaly-looking, becoming bright red and sweet when mature. Each strawberry is elliptical to egg-shaped, about 1 cm in diameter, and has soft flesh with tiny seeds (achenes) that are characteristically raised on the surface.

HABITAT: This native plant grows from lowland to subalpine elevations. In Alberta, it occurs throughout the northern and central parts of the province, extending as far south as Red Deer and Jasper. It is found in moister and shadier areas than other wild strawberries, including open forests, clearings, open slopes, meadows, grasslands and by trails and roadsides.

Cloudberry
syn. Bakeapple

► berries are tart but pleasant.
► berry is finger-wide to thumb-wide.
► plant can reach lower-shin height.

EATING: the berries are edible raw, though they may cause diarrhea or stomach cramps if eaten in quantity. They have a pleasantly sour taste that becoming sweeter as they ripen. They are used in making pies, wines and liquor, and are harvested commercially for use in juices, jams and preserves by Scandinavians. The berries contain high amounts of vitamin C and are also rich in benzoic acid, which allows them to be stored for long periods of time without spoiling. The

berries were cherished by the Inuit, who stored them by freezing them in the snow or placing them in sealskin bags with seal oil. "Eskimo Ice Cream" was traditionally made by combining the berries with seal oil and chewed caribou fat and beating the mixture to a fluffy consistency. The flower are edible raw and both the flowers and leaves (fresh or dried) can be used to make a tea.

DESCRIPTION: This multi-stemmed, perennial herb rarely grows higher than a person's lower shin (25 cm). The wiry annual stems are horizontal to erect, range from green to brownish red, may be slightly hairy and lacks thorns or bristles.

Each stem bears 1–3 green, wrinkly **LEAVES**. The leaves are round to kidney-shaped, indented at the stem, and have 5–7 shallow, rounded lobes. The leaf blade is rarely more than finger-wide (8 cm) and is slightly shorter than it is wide, with edges that are bluntly to sharply toothed. The upper surface is hairless or thinly hairy and the paler underside is hairier, particularly near the veins. The leaves rest on stalks that are about as long as the blades and are alternately arranged on the stem.

In the early summer, a solitary white **FLOWER** is produced at the top of the stem, with male and female flowers occurring on separate plants. The flower is about an inch (2 cm) wide and has five white, spreading, egg-shaped petals that are sometimes red-tipped. The petals surround numerous antenna-like stamens, or pistils in the case of female flowers. Below the petals are five small, green triangular sepals. In the late summer, the female flower develops into a sweetly tart **CLOUDBERRY** that rests atop the stem. Each cloudberry is red and hard when young, turning translucent amber or yellow as it ripens. The "berry" is actually an aggregate of 6–18 drupelets, similar in shape and width to a raspberry (1–2 cm), but with fewer drupelets. Soon after ripening, the cloudberry drops from the stalk.

HABITAT: This native plant grows from lowland to montane elevations in wetter sites of the boreal forest as well as alpine or arctic tundra. In Alberta it occurs at latitudes north of Edmonton, extending south into the areas around Jasper. It can be found in bogs, freshwater marshes and mossy or peaty forest, especially where there is sunny exposure.

Creeping Raspberry

syn. Five-Leaved Bramble,
Strawberryleaf Raspberry

- ▶ berries are sweetish.
- ▶ berry is up to 1 cm wide.
- ▶ plant grows to ankle height.

EATING: The berries are sweetish with moderate flavor. Because they are small and soft, they are difficult to gather or carry in large number, but can be added to jams, jellies, pies, and other baked goods. The Haida traditionally mixed them with Bog cranberries and cooked them for a prolonged time. The flowers are edible raw and can be used as a potherb. The leaves can be dried to make a tea.

DESCRIPTION: The plant is a creeping perennial that grows ankle-high (20 cm) and forms loose mats on the forest floor. The slender, creeping stems, which can reach about 1 m in length, form roots from where the leaves attach and send up erect flowering shoots. The stems and shoots are free of prickles or bristles and are hairless or sparsely hairy.

The **LEAVES** are compound, consisting of five short-stalked leaflets that are radially arranged, earning this plant the common name "Five-leaved bramble". Each leaflet is egg-shaped to diamond-shaped, tapered at the base, and rounded at the end. The leaflet blade is no more than few centimeters long and has edges that are coarsely sharp-toothed. The upper surface is smooth and the underside is hairy, particularly on the veins. The compound leaves have long stalks and are alternately arranged on the stem.

In late spring or early summer, solitary white **FLOWERS** come into bloom at the ends of erect shoots. The flower are at about the same height as the leaves. Each flower is no more than thumb-wide (2 cm) and has five oval, spreading petals that are somewhat down turned when fully open. The petals surround numerous antenna-like stamens. Immediately beneath the petals are five green, pointed sepals that are sparsely hairy and bend backwards. In the late summer, the flowers develop into shiny, bright red **RASPBERRIES**. As with the common raspberry, each "berry" is actually an aggregate of drupelets clustered around a receptacle, which remains behind when they are picked. The berries have characteristically few drupelets—no more than six—with some having only 1–2. A typical berry is about 1 cm wide and has a juicy pulp with a moderate flavor.

HABITAT: This native plant grows from lowland to subalpine elevations. In Alberta, it occurs in the western half of the province as far north as Lesser Slave Lake. It can be found in moist, mossy woods, forest clearings, stream banks and the on the edges of bogs.

Dwarf Red Raspberry

syn. Dwarf Red Blackberry, Dewberry,

▶ berries are sweet.
▶ berry is under 1 cm wide.
▶ plant is shin-high.

EATING: This small, delicate berry is sweet and has a delicious flavor. It does not store or carry well in containers due to its softness and is best eaten when picked. The berries were used by Native American peoples in a manner similar to other raspberries. The Iroquois mashed the raw or cooked berries and spread them on a mat to dry in the sun or next to the fire. The small cakes that they dried into were stored for later use.

DESCRIPTION: The plant is a multi-stemmed, deciduous perennial. The stems creep along the ground and have flowering shoots that branch off, ascending to shin-height (35 cm) and eventually reclining. The stems are reddish brown, softly hairy and only a few millimeters thick, becoming slightly woody near the base. At regular intervals along the horizontal stems, roots emerge. These stems grow up to one meter in length, acquiring a whip-like form. The stems that ascend have erect, leafy branches which, like the stems, lack thorns or bristles.

The thin **LEAVES** are compound, consisting of 3–5 thin, green leaflets that are arranged across from each other, except for the single terminating leaflet. Each leaflet is oval-shaped with a tapering end and a pointed tip. The blade of the leaflet is no longer than a pinky finger (2–6 cm), with edges that are coarsely toothed except near the base. The upper surface is smooth to hairy and the underside is somewhat hairy, particularly on the veins. The terminal leaflet is slightly longer and more diamond-shaped than the others, which are skewed towards the center rather than being symmetrical. The compound leaf has a hairy stalk that is about as long as a leaflet. The leaves are alternately arranged, with 2–5 occurring on each flowering stem.

In the early summer, white (sometimes pinkish) **FLOWERS** emerge in loose clusters of 1–3 at the ends of branches. Each flower is no more than finger wide and has five white, spoon-shaped petals. The petals surround numerous antenna-like stamens that are capped with pale yellow anthers. Directly beneath the petals are five green, triangular sepals that bend backwards. By the late summer, the flowers have developed into reddish purple **RASPBERRIES**. Each "berry" is actually an aggregate of small drupelets arranged around a receptacle, from which the berry does not easily detach. The raspberry is under 1 cm across, roughly spherical, and has sweet, juicy flesh.

HABITAT: This common plant is native to boreal and arctic regions of North America and Asia. In Alberta it diminishes at latitudes south of Calgary. It can be found in moist woods, swamps, low, boggy land and by streams and shorelines.

Arctic Raspberry

syn. Arctic Bramble, Arctic Blackberry, Nagoon Berry

- ▶ berries are delicious.
- ▶ berry is about 1 cm wide.
- ▶ plant grows to boot-height.

EATING: This berry is remarkably sweet and tasty, with a fragrance similar to pineapple. Those who are fortunate enough to gather them in quantity make them into jams, jellies, preserves, pies and other baked goods. In Alaska, the berries were traditionally fried in grease along with dried fish eggs. They were sometimes mixed with grease and stored underground in a birch bark basket. The flowers are edible raw and have a sweet, flavorful taste. The leaves can be used to make a tea, either by drying them or using them fresh.

DESCRIPTION: This multi-stemmed perennial herb rarely exceeds boot height (15 cm) and often forms small, open colonies. The stems, which rise from horizontal underground roots (rhizomes), are pinkish green, just over 1 mm thick, and are occasionally woody at the base. The annual flowering shoots are covered in soft, fine hairs and lack thorns or bristles.

The stems bear numerous compound **LEAVES**, which consist of three short-stalked, greenish leaflets. Each leaflet is egg-shaped to diamond-shaped, narrowing towards the base and having a rounded end. The leaflet blade is no more than half a finger long (4 cm) and is about ¾ as wide, with edges that are often reddish and are coarsely toothed, except near the base. The upper surface is smooth to hairy. The paler underside is a dull green and usually hairy, particularly near the raised veins. The terminal leaflet is slightly longer than the two side leaflets, which are skewed towards the center rather than being symmetrical. The compound leaves have hairy stalks that are slightly longer than the leaflets and are alternately arranged, with 2–5 leaves occurring on each flowering shoot.

In the early summer, richly pink, fragrant **FLOWERS** come into bloom, either singly or in erect clusters of 2–3 at the tops of shoots. Each flower is up to an inch (2.5 cm) wide and has five delicate, spoon-shaped petals. The petals surround 30–50 antenna-like stamens that are yellow to pink and capped with yellowish anthers. Immediately beneath the petals are five slightly shorter, green, narrow, pointed sepals that bend backwards. In the late summer, the flowers develop into deeply red, tasty **RASPBERRIES** that are about 1 cm wide. Each raspberry consists of 15–30 drupelets arranged around a receptacle, from which they separate when they are picked.

HABITAT: This native plant grows from lowland to alpine elevations throughout the western half of Alberta and at latitudes north of Edmonton. It occurs in open canopy forests, thickets, moist meadows, tundra and in soils rich with organic content, including cold swamps and bogs.

Red Raspberry

- ► berries are delicious.
- ► berry is about 1 cm wide.
- ► young shoots are edible raw.
- ► roots are edible when cooked.
- ► bristly shrub reaches a person's height.

EATING: The berries are sweetly tart and delicious, making them excellent for jams, jellies, pies, etc. They were traditionally eaten fresh, cooked in stews, or preserved a number of ways. After cooking or steaming the berries, the Chippewa Indians would spread them into little cakes to be dried on birch bark. Sometimes the fruit was placed on large mats and dried whole by the sun or by fire. In Alaska, the berries were often preserved in grease and stored underground in birch bark baskets. Young, tender shoots of the plant can be peeled and eaten raw. The shoots are best harvested in the spring, when they emerge from the ground. Intermediate sized roots of the plant are also edible after extensive boiling.

DESCRIPTION: This deciduous shrub is similar to the cultivated raspberry. It rarely grows beyond a person's height (1.8 m) and is about as wide as it is tall. It has round, arching stems (or "canes") that are erect or drooping, often forming dense tangles. Young stems are green, becoming yellowish brown or purple, with older bark becoming brown and shredding off in layers. The canes and branches are armed with fine, straight, narrow, bristly prickles.

The **LEAVES** are compound, consisting of 3–5 green leaflets that are arranged across from each other, except for the single leaflet at the end. Older leaves generally consist of only three leaflets. Each leaflet is egg-shaped and narrows to a sharply pointed tip. The leaflet blade is rarely longer than a finger (8 cm) and has edges that are coarsely toothed. The upper surface is hairless and the underside has a soft, white fuzz that can be almost absent. The compound leaves are alternately arranged.

In the summer, white to greenish **FLOWERS** appear singly or in drooping clusters (cymes) of 2–5. The flowers are up to finger-wide (1.5 cm), emerging from where the leaves attach near the tips of new branchlets. Each flower has five white, spoon-shaped petals that surround 70–100 antenna-like stamens. Beneath and between the petals are five longer, triangular, green sepals that bend backwards. In late summer, the flowers develop into clusters of sweetly tart, red **RASPBERRIES** that are finely hairy. Each raspberry is egg-shaped, up to finger-wide (1.5 cm), and consists of numerous drupelets arranged around central receptacle, from which they fall after ripening.

HABITAT: This native shrub grows from lowland to montane elevations. In Alberta it occurs at latitudes south of Red Deer and throughout the western half of the province, declining north of Grand Prairie. It can be found on rocky slopes, in moist, open forests, clearings and old fields, as well as near stream banks and by roadsides.

Thimbleberry

- ▶ berries have a neutral taste.
- ▶ berry is finger-wide to thumb-wide.
- ▶ spring shoots and flowers are edible raw.
- ▶ shrub grows within a person's reach.

EATING: The berry has a neutral to sweetish taste but is relatively coarse, seedy and thin compared to the more juicy raspberry which it resembles. The ripe berries tend to fall apart when picked, but if gathered in quantity are particularly good for jellies and preserves. They are rich in vitamin C and were widely utilized by native North American Indians. They were usually picked while still pink and allowed to ripen off the bush, since the berries transition from unripe to ripe within a day or two. They were traditionally eaten raw, stewed, or dried into cakes for storage. Emerging spring shoots were gathered in large quantities, peeled, and eaten either raw or cooked. The flowers are edible raw and the leaves were used as a general purpose liner for drying berries, wrapping meat for baking, and for separating layers in steam pits.

DESCRIPTION: The plant is a thornless deciduous shrub with one to several woody stems, usually growing within a person's reach (2.2 m). It is almost as wide as it is tall and often forms dense thickets. The stems are upright, somewhat spindly in form, and are rarely thicker than a finger (1.5 cm). The bark is thin and grayish, becoming shredded or flaky with age. The branches and twigs are green and finely hairy, graying in maturity.

The broad, thin **LEAVES** have 3–5 lobes, similar to a maple leaf, with a base that is indented at the stalk. The leaf blade can be as wide and long as an outstretched hand (10–20 cm), and each triangular lobe is finely but unevenly toothed. The upper and lower surfaces are velvety and dull green, with the underside paler. Mature leaves have finger-long (8 cm) leafstalks covered in red hairs and are alternately arranged on the branch, turning bright orange to burgundy in the fall.

In the early summer, white **FLOWERS** emerge in flat-topped clusters of 2–7 at the tips of branches. The flower is up to a couple inches wide (5 cm) and has five egg-shaped petals that are textured like crinkled tissue paper. The petals spread into a bowl that surrounds numerous pale yellow, antenna-like stamens and pistils. Just beneath the petals are five elongated, triangular, green sepals. In mid to late summer, the flowers develop into clusters of red, slightly hairy **BERRIES** that have a neutral taste and resemble thinned-out, flattened raspberries. As with raspberries, the "berry" is actually an aggregate of closely packed drupelets. It is finger-wide to thumb-wide (1.5–2 cm) and falls from its receptacle when ripe.

HABITAT: This native plant grows from lowland to subalpine elevations, though in Alberta it only occurs in the mountains bordering British Columbia. It can be found on wooded slopes, forest edges, clearings and along stream banks.

False Toadflax

syn. Northern Comandra, Timberberry

- berries are tasteless.
- berry is no more than pea-sized.
- plant grows as high as the lower-shin.

EATING: This berry is reportedly edible, though it is bland tasting. In Alaska it was used for food, and a number of Native American groups including the Cree and Chipewyan utilized the berry, though its uses were largely medicinal: the berries were taken as a remedy for persistent chest problems and the chewed leaves and stem were applied as a poultice for wounds.

DESCRIPTION: This erect, perennial herb grows to lower-shin level (25 cm) and has roots that are parasitic on other plants. The reddish brown stems occur singly or as several and die back every season. They are hairless and have no branches.

The **LEAVES** are elliptical to egg-shaped, narrow at the base and rounded or bluntly pointed at the end. The leaf blade is rarely more than half a pinky finger in length (3 cm). It is just over half as wide as it is long and has smooth edges. The upper surface is bright green, often with yellow streaks or patches and has net-like veins that yellow with age. The underside is a similar in color to the upper surface. The leaves have short stalks and are alternately arranged on the stem, with no leaves occurring where the stem meets the ground.

In the early summer, greenish white **FLOWERS** with slender flower stalks come into bloom. The flowers emerge in clusters (cymes) of three (less often two or four) along the middle and upper stem just above some of the leaves. Each flower is up to ½ cm across and has no petals but rather has five spreading, triangular, petal-like sepals that range in color from light green to purple. The middle flower is usually female, while the two on either side are male and quickly fall away. On male flowers, the sepals surround five antenna-like stamens, while on the female flowers, they surround a single, stubby, rod-like pistil. In the late summer, the middle flower of each cluster has developed into a tasteless, fleshy **BERRY** ranging in color from bright orange to red. The berry is spherical, no more than pea-sized (5–8 mm), and contains a single seed.

HABITAT: This plant grows below subalpine elevations. It is widespread across the boreal forest and has roots that are parasitic on a variety of other plants, including bearberry, heathers, pines, willows and aster. In Alberta it occurs throughout the province, diminishing at latitudes south of High River and eastwards of the line between High River and Vegreville. It can be found in shady coniferous woods, mossy areas, and bogs.

Bastard Toadflax

- ▶ unripe berries are oily, sweet.
- ▶ berry is under 1 cm long.
- ▶ plant grows to upper shin level.

WARNING: Eating the berries in quantity may cause nausea.

EATING: The berries have an oily, but pleasantly sweet taste if they are eaten while still immature (slightly green). When purplish, they remain palatable but are less tasty. Although they are difficult to gather in quantity, several Native American groups made use of their seeds. The Salishan reportedly ate the seeds as a principle food.

DESCRIPTION: The plant is an erect, perennial herb with a variable form, growing as high as upper-shin level (40 cm). The roots are semi-parasitic on the roots of other plants, from which they draw moisture and nutrients. The hairless, rigid stems are light green in color and occur singly or in clusters of 2–7. The stem is no more than ½ cm thick at the almost-woody base and is either branchless or has only a few branches.

The thick **LEAVES** are narrowly elliptical, tapering both at the base and towards the sharply pointed tip. The leaf blade is rarely more than half a finger long (4 cm) and is about a quarter as wide, with edges that are smooth. The upper surface is light grayish green with a dull, powdery appearance and veins that are difficult to discern. The underside appears similar to the upper surface. The leaves have virtually no leafstalks and are alternately arranged, usually inclined or hugging the stem but not occurring where the stem meets the ground.

In the early to midsummer, scentless, greenish white (sometimes pink-tinged) **FLOWERS** emerge in tightly packed, rounded or flat-topped clusters (panicles or corymbs) at the top of the stems. The cluster is a couple inches (5 cm) across and is composed of numerous smaller clusters (cymules) of 3–6 flowers. Each flower is about pea-sized (5–7 mm) and has five narrowly oval, petal-like sepals rather than petals. The sepals fuse into a funnel-shape below and flare outwards at the tips, surrounding five short (1 mm), yellow, antenna-like stamens. In the late summer, the flowers develop into **BERRIES** (actually drupes) that are initially green, becoming light brown with bluish or purplish coloring when mature. The berry is spherical to egg-shaped, under 1 cm long, and consists of a thin layer of dry to fleshy pulp surrounding a large, smooth seed. The berry terminates with the remnants of the dried flower.

HABITAT: The native plant grows from lowland to montane elevations. It occurs throughout Alberta except in the northwest corner bounded by High Level. It can be found in dry, open, pine woods, shrubland, prairie grasslands, foothills, and on sandy to rocky slopes.

Bunchberry

syn. Dwarf/Creeping Dogwood,
Canadian Dwarf Cornel

► berry is bland with crunchy seeds.
► berry is pea-sized.
► plant grows to boot height.

EATING: The berries are bland to mildly sweet and have a mealy, gummy texture. They are edible raw, though eating unripe berries can cause stomach cramps. The berries are popular for making pies and puddings. They are high in pectin and can be mixed with other low-pectin berries to make jams or jellies. The berries were traditionally gathered in quantity by a number of Native American peoples and either eaten raw, dried for winter use, or mixed with fish grease and eaten as a dessert.

DESCRIPTION: The plant is an erect, perennial herb that typically grows to boot height (5–15 cm), often forming large colonies that carpet the ground. The slender, green to reddish stems are unbranched and 2-grooved. The lower stem has a few pairs of small, scale-like leaves arranged across from each other.

At the top of the stem is a ring of 4–6 arching, papery **LEAVES** on a short (1–2 mm) leaf stalk. The leaves are elliptical to diamond shaped, tapering at both ends and ending with a pointed tip. If occurring as four, the leaves are a similar size. Otherwise, four smaller leaves typically form a ring just above two larger leaves that are directly across from each other. The leaf blades are no more than finger-long (4–8 cm), have smooth edges and whitish undersides. Several pairs of veins branch from the midvein on the lower half and run down the leaf in parallel.

Just above the leaves rests what appears to be a single, 4-petalled white **FLOWER** a few centimeters across. This "flower" is actually an arrangement of four white, petal-like bracts surrounding a dense, umbrella-shaped cluster (compound cyme) of 10–25 tiny flowers that range from greenish-white to purple. Each flower is about 2 mm wide and has four white petals that bend backwards. Between the petals are four longer, white, spreading, antenna-like stamens capped with pale yellow anthers. The flowers appear from late spring to midsummer. By late summer, the flowers develop into a dense cluster of bright red, mild-tasting **BERRIES** (actually drupes). The berry is less than 1 cm wide and contains a crunchy, egg-shaped stone which does not separate easily from the yellow flesh.

HABITAT: This common, native plant grows from lowland to subalpine elevations throughout Alberta. It can be found in the shady understory of conifer forests, mossy areas and moist habitats. It often grows on the sides of large, decaying stumps or tree trunks.

Wild Lily-of-the-valley

syn. Canada Mayflower

- ▶ berries are tart.
- ▶ berry is about half a centimeter wide.
- ▶ plant grows to boot height.

WARNING: Although the berries of this species are not considered poisonous, they are also not widely eaten. A closely related European species (*M. bifolium*) is known to contain cardiotonic glucosides and saponins, which are capable of causing serious nervous and cardiac disorders. The berries are not recommended except as a trail side nibble.

EATING: The fully ripe, red berries are fleshy and tart, with a flavor reminiscent of cranberries. They are a good source of vitamin C, but are only suitable for eating in small amounts, since they are a known cathartic (i.e., they accelerate defecation). The berries were not widely utilized by Indigenous peoples. The Forest Potawatomi Indians of Wisconsin reportedly ate them, but the details of their traditional preparation and usage are unclear.

DESCRIPTION: This erect, perennial herb grows boot-high (15 cm), often forming colonies in scattered clumps or large patches of single-leaved shoots. The stout, green stem is unbranched below the flowers and somewhat crooked, zig-zagging at each of its 1–2 (occasionally three) leaves.

The **LEAF** is egg-shaped, indented at the stem and tapers towards a blunt or pointed tip. The leaf blade is finger-long (3–8 cm) and about ⅔ as wide, with smooth edges and parallel veins running from the base to the tip. The upper surface is smooth and the underside may have fine hairs. The leaves are alternately arranged on the stem, with the larger lower leaves having virtually no leafstalk and clasping the stem, while the upper leaves have short (<1 cm) leafstalks.

In the late spring or early summer, some of the plants develop fragrant, starry, white **FLOWERS**. The flowers emerge in an erect, cylindrical cluster (raceme) of 10–40 at the top of the stem. Within the cluster, the stalk is characteristically straight rather than zig-zagging and the flowers occur in pairs. Each flower measures under 1 cm across and characteristically has four creamy white petals. The petals are narrowly oval, have blunted tips and bend strongly backwards, making them rather inconspicuous. They surround four thick, white, antenna-like stamens that spread outwards beyond the petals. The stamens are capped with pale yellow anthers. By the late summer, **BERRIES** that were initially hard and light green become mottled brown/red and then red, soft, and somewhat translucent. Some varieties are speckled pink or red at maturity. Each berry is spherical, about ½ cm wide, and has tart flesh that contains 1–2 small, round, dark brown seeds.

HABITAT: This widespread, native plant grows from lowland to montane elevations at latitudes north of Red Deer. It can be found in the understory of the boreal forest and in forest clearings.

False Solomon's Seal

syn. False Lily-of-the-valley, Treacleberry Solomon's Plume, False Spikenard,

► berries are bittersweet.
► berry is pea-sized.
► plant grows to waist height.

EATING: The ripe berries have an arguably pleasant taste reminiscent of bitter molasses but may act as a laxative, particularly when raw. Though they are not commonly collected by berry pickers, they have a good shelf-life and can be used in jams and jellies. The Thompson Indians collected the berries in large quantities for food. The young leaves are edible raw or cooked. The young shoots can be stripped of leaves, cooked and eaten like asparagus, though it is not recommended due to the similarity with poisonous shoots of False Hellebore (*Veratrum viride*). The root can be also cooked and eaten as one would a potato, though it is poor-tasting unless soaked in lye.

DESCRIPTION: The plant is an upright perennial herb that grows to waist height (90 cm). The slightly hairy stem is green and erect when young, becoming reddish brown and sometimes stiffly arching when larger. The stem does not branch, but bends slightly where each leaf is attached, terminating with a cluster of flowers or berries atop the stem.

The **LEAVES** are elliptical to egg-shaped with a rounded base that clasps the stem and gradually taper to a tip. The leaf blade is rarely more than hand-length (17 cm) and is about half as wide as it is long. It has smooth edges and heavy veins that run parallel to each other down to the tip. The upper surface is smooth and the underside is finely hairy. The leaves are alternately arranged along the stem, forming a row on either side.

In the early summer, tiny, sweet-smelling, white **FLOWERS** emerge in a tight, branching cluster (panicle) at the end of the stem. The feathery-looking cluster is about as long as a pen (12 cm) and pyramid-shaped. It contains 50–250 flowers that rest on short flower stalks, blooming from the bottom up. Each flower is under ½ cm across and has six narrow, white petals. The petals surround six longer and wider, antenna-like stamens that are white and capped with yellowish anthers. The flowers develop into a dense cluster of **BERRIES** that are initially mottled green and copper, becoming entirely red when mature in the late summer. Each berry is pea-sized (5–7 mm) and roughly spherical, but often has three hump-shaped lobes. The bittersweet pulp contains 1–2 seeds.

HABITAT: This common native plant grows from lowland to subalpine elevations. In Alberta it occurs at longitudes west of Edmonton as far north as High Level. It can be found in moist, rich woods, forest clearings, thickets, and by rivers and streambanks.

Star-flowered False Solomon's Seal

syn. Starry False Lily-of-the-valley

- ▶ berries are bittersweet.
- ▶ berry is about 1 cm wide.
- ▶ young leaves are edible raw.
- ▶ shoots can be cooked like asparagus.
- ▶ plant grows below knee height.

EATING: The berries are bittersweet and contain enough vitamin C to have been used in preventing scurvy. In those who are unaccustomed, however, they can have a laxative effect, especially when eaten raw. A number of coastal peoples including the Thompson Indians collected the berries in quantity for food. The young leaves are edible raw and the young shoots can be stripped of leaves, cooked and eaten similar to asparagus. The root can be cooked and eaten as one would a potato, though it is poor-tasting unless soaked in lye.

DESCRIPTION: This ascending, perennial herb usually grows below knee-height (50 cm), often in dense clusters. The slightly hairy, round stem is green and erect when young, often becoming reddish at the base and reclining or arching stiffly when larger. It is no more than ½ cm thick at the base and has no branches, but bends slightly at each leaf, giving it a slight zig-zag appearance.

The **LEAVES** are narrowly elongated with a rounded base that usually clasps the stem, tapering gradually to a pointed tip and sometimes folding along the midvein to create a trough. The leaf blade is rarely more than pen-long (13 cm) and up to a third as wide, with smooth edges and 3–5 prominent, parallel veins that run down to the tip. The upper surface is smooth and the underside is finely hairy. The leaves have virtually no stalks and are alternately arranged along the stem, usually in an ascending orientation. They are relatively closely spaced and forming a row on either side of the stem.

For about three weeks starting in the late spring, star-shaped, creamy white **FLOWERS** appear in a narrow, loose cluster (raceme) at the top of the stem. The cluster can be finger-long (8 cm) and consists of 5–15 flowers. Each flower is up to 1 cm across and has six narrow, spreading petals that surround six antenna-like stamens capped with yellowish anthers. The flowers have a mild fragrance and rest on flower stalks about 1 cm long. By the fall, the flowers have developed into clusters of 2–8 **BERRIES** that are initially light yellow with three purplish stripes, becoming completely purplish red or reddish black when mature. The berry is roughly spherical or has three hump-shaped lobes, is about 1 cm wide, and has a bittersweet pulp that contains 1–6 light brown, bluntly triangular seeds.

HABITAT: This native plant grows from lowland to subalpine elevations, declining at latitudes north of High Level. It can be found in moist woods, clearings, thickets, and on stream banks. It also occurs in open, sandy places, including prairies, shorelines, and sand dunes.

21

Claspleaf Twisted-stalk

syn. White/Clasping Twisted-stalk,
Wild cucumber, Watermelon Berry,

► berries are bland.
► berry is about 1 cm wide.
► leaves and roots are edible raw.
► plant grows to waist height.

EATING: The ripe berry is juicy and has a bland, cucumber flavor that is shared by the leaves, roots, and the young shoots, all of which are edible raw or cooked. The leaves and roots of mature plants are suitable for cooking or use a potherb; however, the young shoots can resemble poisonous members of the genus *Veratrum* and are not recommended. Early settlers referred to berries "scoot berries" for the laxative (cathartic) effect they can have when eaten in quantity. Native groups considered the berries to be inedible,.

DESCRIPTION: This erect perennial herb grows no more than waist high (1 m). The stem branches widely below the middle and has a crooked, zig-zagging appearance due to regular, sharp kinks that occur along its length at every leaf. The stem is green and is either completely smooth or covered with short, rigid, reddish hairs on the lower third.

The **LEAVES** are narrowly elliptical, tapering to a pointy tip. They lack leafstalks, instead having a base that is indented where it encircles around to clasp the stem, hence the common name "Claspleaf." The leaf blade is up to half a foot (5–15 cm) long and is usually less than half as wide, with edges that are either smooth or lined with minute, irregularly spaced teeth. The upper surface is green and has parallel veins running to the tip, whereas the underside is more grayish. The leaves are alternately arranged on the stem.

In the early summer, bell-shaped **FLOWERS** ranging from white to green-tinged emerge along the stem, hanging singly (or sometimes as two) from the lower side of each leaf. The flower stalks have a characteristic, sharp kink that is closer to the flower. Each flower is about 1 cm long and has six distinct petals (actually tepals) that bend strongly backwards. The petals form a bell that surrounds six short, antenna-like stamens. The stamens are unequal in length and are capped with long, pointed anthers that protrude past the petals. By the late summer or early fall, the flowers develop into almost-round or elongated, juicy **BERRIES.** The berries are initially greenish and resemble tiny watermelons, turning yellow and finally red when ripe. They have a smooth, tender skin and mild taste. Each berry hangs from a characteristically sharp-kinked stem, is about 1 cm wide and somewhat longer, and contains several small (3 mm), grooved seeds.

HABITAT: This common native plant grows from lowland to sub-alpine elevations at latitudes north and longitudes west of Edmonton, diminishing at latitudes north of High Level. It can be found in moist, shaded forests and clearings, often in dense undergrowth and near streams.

Rosy Twisted-stalk

syn. Rose Twisted-stalk, Rose Mandarin,
Rosybells, Scootberry.

- ▶ berries are bland.
- ▶ berry is under 1 cm wide.
- ▶ leaves are edible.
- ▶ plant grows below knee-level.

EATING: The raw berry is bland to sweetish, with a taste similar to cucumber. Eaten in quantity, the berries may have a laxative (cathartic) effect. The young leaves are suitable as a potherb. The Cherokee cooked them by boiling and frying.

DESCRIPTION: The plant is an erect perennial herb typically growing below knee-level (50 cm). The finely hairy, green stem is usually unbranched, though older plants may have one or two branches. Where each leafstalk attaches, the stem has a fringe of fine hairs and a slight kink or bend that gives it a mildly crooked appearance.

The **LEAVES** are narrowly elliptical, taper to a pointed tip, and have a rounded base. The leaves lack stalks but the base of the leaf does not wrap around the stem. The leaf blade is usually no more than palm-length (10 cm) and is less than half as wide. The edges of the blade are not toothed but are characteristically lined with short, spiky hairs. The upper and lower surface are shiny, hairless and have clearly parallel veins that run to the tip. The leaves are alternately arranged but absent on the lower part of the stem.

In the late spring or early summer, solitary (or rarely, paired) bell-shaped **FLOWERS** emerge from where the leaves attach, ranging in color from rosy pink to purple-streaked. Each flower is about 1 cm long and hangs below the leaf on a flower stalk that is characteristically curved near the middle. The scientific name, which roughly translates to "Twisted Stalk", refers to this bend. The flower has six distinct petals (actually tepals) that flare at their whitish, pointed tips. The petals form a bell that surrounds six non-protruding, antenna-like stamens capped with double-pointed anthers. By the fall, the flowers have developed into bright red to purplish **BERRIES** that are roughly spherical (not elongated) and hang from characteristically curved (but not sharply kinked) stems. The berry is less than 1 cm wide and has a juicy pulp that has a mild taste and contains small (3 mm), whitish seeds.

HABITAT: This native plant grows from lowland to subalpine elevations. In western Alberta, it occurs in the foothills and uplands of the Rocky Mountains. It can be found in cool, moist, shaded forests and clearings, often in the dense undergrowth where there are rich, moist soils.

Hooker's Fairybells
syn. Drops-of-gold

- ▶ berries are bland.
- ▶ berry is about 1 cm long.
- ▶ plant can grow to waist-height.

EATING: The raw berry is bland to sweet. Though considered edible, as a member of the Lily family it may be mildly toxic and cause diarrhea or stomach cramps if eaten in large quantities. It was occasionally used for food by the Thompson Indians of British Columbia, but was not considered an important food. It is suitable for foraging in small quantities as a trail-side nibble.

DESCRIPTION: This upright, perennial herb can grow to waist-height (90 cm). It has several to many slender, arching stems. The stems are straw-colored, tending to fork into a few horizontally spreading branches above the middle. The upper stem in particular is covered with fuzzy hairs.

The thin, papery **LEAVES** are narrowly elongated or egg-shaped, taper to a sharply pointed tip, and have bases that are either round or indented at the base. They lack stalks and clasp the stem slightly. The leaf blade about palm-length (10 cm) though it can grow to half a foot (15 cm). It is just under half as wide as it is long and has sometimes rough edges that can be somewhat wavy or irregularly curled. The upper surface is dull green and hairless to sparsely hairy with prominent veins that run down the leaf in parallel. The underside is rougher and hairier, especially along the edges and on the veins. The leaves are alternately arranged. The blades are oriented horizontally to the ground and the upper leaves are typically angled relative to the stem.

In the late spring or early summer, narrowly bell-shaped **FLOWERS** come into bloom, ranging from creamy white to greenish or yellowish. The flowers emerge in clusters of 1–3 (usually two), dangling from the stem-tips. The flowers may be difficult to spot from above when they are hidden by the cover of leaves. Each flower is no longer than thumb-width (2 cm) and has six veiny petals (actually tepals) that are elongated and bluntly pointed, flaring outwards at their tips. The petals surround six antenna-like stamens that are capped with large, bulbous anthers, sometimes protruding past the mouth of the bell. The common name "Fairybell" refers to the fairylike nature of the flowers.

In the late summer, the flowers develop into smooth or minutely hairy **BERRIES** that are initially dark yellow, becoming orange to bright red when mature. The berries are broadly egg-shaped and about 1 cm long. They have a bland tasting pulp that contains 4–6 seeds, each about ½ cm long. The common name "Drops of Gold" refers to the initial golden color of the berries.

HABITAT: This native plant grows in lowland and upland elevations in moderately moist areas. In Alberta it occurs in the southern half of the province, often in areas removed from roads and trails. It can be found in damp, shady forests, wooded ravines and on riverbanks.

Roughfruit Fairybells

syn. Rough-fruited Mandarin

- ▶ berries are mealy and bland.
- ▶ berry is about 1 cm wide.
- ▶ plant grows to knee level.

EATING: The berries have a leathery, mealy texture and flavor that range from tasteless to slightly sweet and reminiscent of apricot. The berries were traditionally gathered and eaten fresh by a number of tribes, including the Blackfoot and Shuswap Indians. There were considered less desirable than the Saskatoon berry or Chokecherries, which often grow in the same locales.

DESCRIPTION: The plant is an erect, perennial herb that often grows about a foot (30 cm) high, though it can reach just over knee level (60 cm). The stems are hairless or have short hair. At regular intervals along the stem are drooping branches that are brown and woody-looking.

The soft **LEAVES** are egg-shaped with a base that is round or heart-shaped and clasps the stem tightly. They are widest at the base and taper to a pointed tip. The leaf blade is rarely more than finger-long (8 cm) and just over half as wide, with edges that lack teeth but are fringed with fine, spreading hairs. The upper surface is smooth and has about seven veins that run down the leaf in parallel, a few of which are prominently impressed. The underside is softly hairy, especially near the base and on the edges. The leaves lack stalks and are alternately arranged on the stem, maintaining a horizontal orientation.

In the late spring or early summer, bell-shaped **FLOWERS** come into bloom, ranging from creamy white to greenish and without markings. The flowers emerge in clusters of 1–3 (usually two), dangling at the branch tips. They are often obscured the cover of leaves and only open briefly before vanishing. Each flower is no longer than a thumb width (2 cm) and has six petals (actually tepals) that are elongated and bluntly pointed, forming a bell-shape that flares outward from about the middle. The petals surround six yellow, antenna-like stamens that are capped with large, bulbous anthers, usually protruding beyond the bell. By the late summer, the flowers develop into velvety, squatly spherical **BERRIES**. The berries are initially green, turning orange and finally bright red when mature. They are about 1 cm wide and have a velvety, bumpy outer surface that is often warty or roughened, earning them the common name "Roughfruit". The pulp is mealy and bland-tasting, and contains 6–12 seeds, each of which are up to ½ cm long.

HABITAT: This common native plant grows from prairie to montane zones. It occurs throughout Alberta, diminishing at latitudes north of Fort McMurray and south of the line between Calgary and Lloydminster. It can be found in moist, shady woods, forest clearings, thickets, woodland edges, and in rich soil by streams.

Utah Honeysuckle

syn. Red Twinberry, Fly Honeysuckle

► berries have a mild, juicy flavor.
► berry is pea-sized.
► shrub grows as tall as a person.

EATING: These juicy, mild tasting berries do not normally attract the attention of serious berry pickers, partly because the shrubs are distributed sparsely and the berries are difficult to gather in large quantities. Even so, they can be eaten fresh or used in cooking, and are said to make an excellent jelly. They were traditionally collected for food by some Native American groups, including the Okanagan-Colville. Their juiciness makes them a possible source of emergency water.

DESCRIPTION: The plant is an upright, deciduous shrub that rarely grows taller than a person (1.8 m) and often has a clumpy form. The erect to leaning stems have a reddish gray bark that is dotted with lighter-colored pockmarks (lenticels) and becomes grayer and slightly shredded with age. The slender, wide-spreading branches are arranged across from each other. Twigs of the current season are green and smooth, becoming reddish gray. They have solid centers (piths) and bear small, stout, pointed buds with purplish bud scales.

The thin **LEAVES** are elliptical to egg-shaped, rounded at the end, and have a base that is round or indented at the leafstalk. The leaf blade is rarely more than a couple inches (5 cm) long and is over half as wide. The edges of the blade lack teeth but are often slightly hairy, especially near the base. The upper surface is bright green and hairless, while the slightly paler underside usually has scattered hairs. The leaves have short (5 mm) stalks and are arranged across from each other on the branch.

In the spring or early summer, trumpet-shaped **FLOWERS** ranging from white to pale yellow come into bloom. The flowers hang downward in pairs from where the leaves attach. The flower pair occurs at the end of a flower stalk that is up to an inch (2.5 cm) long. Each flower is no more than a couple centimeters long. It consists of five lobes that form a floral tube whose base is conspicuously swollen on one side. Within the tube are five antenna-like stamens capped with yellow anthers and a slightly longer, rod-like pistil that protrudes past the flaring mouth. Immediately below the flowers there may be a pair (involucre) of very small, slender, leaf-like bracts that are arranged across from each other. Beginning in the summer and continuing until the fall, the flowers develop into pairs of bright, reddish orange **BERRIES** that are joined at the base. Each berry is spherical or slightly tapering, about pea-sized (5–8 mm), and has mild-tasting, juicy flesh containing 2–4 seeds.

HABITAT: This common, native shrub grows from lowland to subalpine elevations. In Alberta, it occurs in subalpine areas in the most southwestern tip of the province. It can be found in the understory of open forests, shrublands and in wetlands, including bogs and along streams.

Northern Red Currant

syn. Wild/Swamp Red Currant,

- ► berries are sour but palatable.
- ► berry is pea-sized.
- ► shrub reaches waist height.

EATING: The berries are sour but palatable when eaten raw, and have a flavor similar to the cultivated red currants found in gardens. They are high in pectin, making them suitable for jams and jellies and are a popular additions to pies, cakes, and other baked goods. They can be sprinkled in salads, and are an interesting substitute for vinegar in vinaigrettes. Native Americans ate the berries fresh or dried them in the sun or by the fire. Cooked berries were also mashed into cakes and dried for later use.

DESCRIPTION: This straggly shrub has one to several erect or reclining stems that are clustered together, rarely growing beyond waist height (90 cm). The stem is no more than 1 cm thick and is covered in grayish to purplish brown bark that can become shredded at the base. The branches are lax and have no thorns or bristles. The young branches are smooth and grayish, with new twigs light green. The lowest branches often creep along the ground and form roots.

The **LEAVES** occur in clusters of 2–5 on short shoots, forming horizontal layers of foliage. Each leaf have 3–5 triangular lobes, similar to a maple-leaf (but more shallowly lobed), and has a base that is slightly indented at the stem. The thin leaf blade grows to palm-size (10 cm), is slightly wider that it is long, and has edges that are coarsely toothed. The upper surface is smooth and the has five main veins that are raised on the underside of the blade. The leaves rest on stalks that are about as long as the blades. They are alternately arranged.

In late spring or early summer, saucer-shaped **FLOWERS** emerge, ranging from greenish to purple-tinged. They are arranged in elongated, drooping clusters (racemes) of 6–20, the cluster being as long as a leaf. Each flower is about ½ cm wide and has five rounded petal-like sepals that form a saucer. Within are five tiny, inconspicuous petals and five stubby, antenna-like stamens capped with yellowish anthers. In the late summer, the flowers develop into dangling clusters of bright, translucent red berries that are hard and smooth. Each **BERRY** is spherical, about pea-sized (5–7 mm) and has a juicy, sour pulp that contains 2–4 tan, oval, seeds that are flattened. The berries are characteristically upturned on their stems and terminate with a short, wick-like remnant of the dried flower.

HABITAT: This native plant grows from lowland to montane elevations. In Alberta, it occurs at latitudes north of Edmonton and throughout the western half of the province to latitudes as far south as Red Deer. It can be found in cool, wet woods, lake shores, and the margins of swamps and bogs. At montane and subalpine elevations, it can be found on rocky slopes and in rock slides.

27

Golden Currant

syn. Clove Currant, Missouri Currant, Buffalo Currant.

▶ berries are tartly sweet, flavorful.
▶ berry is pea-sized.
▶ thornless shrub grows within arm's reach.

EATING: The berries are tartly sweet, seedy, and quite flavorful compared to other currants. They contain high levels of pectin, making them popular in jams and jellies. They are also used to make sauces, wines, pies, desserts, and other baked goods. The berries were used by a number of Native American groups, who would dry them for storage or make pemmican by combining them with other berries, grease, and meat. The dried berries were sometimes pounded, ground and formed into cakes or combined with seed flour for making a mush. The sweet-tasting flowers are edible raw.

DESCRIPTION: This deciduous shrub usually grows within arm's reach (2.3 m) and has a spread roughly equivalent to its height. The erect, woody stems are covered in dark, silvery gray bark and lack spines or thorns. The many branches are smooth and stiff. The twigs are reddish gray and have reddish brown, pointed buds.

The **LEAVES** have three deep, round lobes and a base that ranges from flat or abruptly tapered to indented at the leafstalk. Each lobe may have several large, blunt teeth at the end. The leaf blade is up to half a finger long (4 cm) and is slightly wider than long. The semi-glossy upper surface is light green color and may be slightly hairy, particularly on younger leaves. The underside is paler than the upper surface. The leaves rest on leafstalks that are up to several centimeters long. They are alternately arranged, occurring in clusters on short side-branchlets, and turn red in the autumn.

In the spring, golden yellow, trumpet-shaped **FLOWERS** emerge, inspiring the common name "Golden Currant." The flowers occur in clusters (racemes) of 5–18 from short, leafy, branchlets and have a fragrance reminiscent of cloves or vanilla. Each flower is no longer than finger width (15 mm). The mouth of the floral tube abruptly flares out into five spreading, yellow, rounded lobes. From within emerge five small, erect petals that are often red-tipped. The petals surround five short, antenna-like stamens that are capped with white anthers. The flower stalks are almost as long as the flowers. By mid to late summer, the flowers have developed into hanging clusters of glossy, bittersweet **BERRIES** or "currants" that are initially green, becoming red or black (rarely orange or yellow) when mature. The berry is spherical, pea-sized (6–8 mm), and contains numerous seeds. It terminates with the dried, brown remnant of the flowerhead.

HABITAT: In Alberta, this plant occurs in the southeastern quadrant of the province roughly bound by Drumheller. It can be found in grasslands, woods, ravines, and along streams.

Skunk Currant

syn. White Currant

- ▶ berries are tart to unpalatable.
- ▶ berry is pea-sized.
- ▶ shrub grows waist-high.

EATING: The berries are juicy and range in taste from sweetly tart to unpalatable, depending on the location and growing conditions. Though they have a skunky odor when crushed, they are used to make jams and are sold commercially in Quebec as a compote. The Woods Cree and the Algonquin traditionally collected the raw berries in quantity as a food source. White currant is a cultivar of this species and is used commercially in preserves, wines, syrups and is also the main ingredient in Bar-le-duc, a well-regarded French jelly.

DESCRIPTION: This straggly, deciduous shrub reaches waist-height (1 m) and emits a skunky odor when bruised. The thin (5 mm) stems are erect to leaning and have grayish bark that becomes reddish brown around the base on older plants. A thin set of ridges run along the stems, which are loosely branched. The branches are smooth, brown to reddish gray and either ascend or trail along the ground.

The **LEAVES** have 5–7 pointed lobes, similar to a maple leaf, and are indented at the stem. The leaf blade is no more than finger-long (8 cm) and about as wide, with edges that are coarsely toothed or double-toothed. The upper surface is shiny and hairless, and the paler under-side is shiny and sparsely hairy near the five main veins. The leaves rest on stems that are almost as long as the blades. They are alternately arranged and often occur in small clusters.

In the late spring or early summer, saucer-shaped, white **FLOWERS** emerge in erect, loose clusters (racemes) at the ends of short, leafy shoots. Each cluster consists of 5–15 flowers and is no longer than a pinky finger (6 cm). The flower is under 1 cm wide and has five white, egg-shaped, petal-like sepals that form a shallow cup. Between the sepals are inconspicuous, pinkish petals that are egg-shaped and under 1 mm long. The petals surround five short, red, antenna-like stamens capped with pink anthers. By late summer, the flowers develop into upright clusters of shiny, brownish red berries that are translucent and covered in red bristly hairs. These hairs are the stalked glands referred to by the scientific name. Each **BERRY** is almost spherical, about pea-sized (6–8 mm), and has juicy, often unpleasant tasting pulp that contains small (2 mm) seeds. The White currant, which is a cultivar of this species, is similar in most respects but has white berries.

HABITAT: This plant occurs throughout the western half of Alberta at latitudes south of Ft. McMurray and occurs in the eastern half at latitudes north of Edmonton. It can be found in cool, moist woods, clearings, thickets, rocky slopes, and by roadways.

Lowbush Cranberry

syn. Squashberry, Mooseberry

► berries have a tart, acidic taste.
► berry is about 1 cm across.
► bush can exceed arm's reach.

WARNING: The raw berries should be eaten in moderation to avoid stomach upset. Spit out the seeds and the tough skin.

EATING: The raw berries are juicy, musky-smelling, and very tart, though their flavor improves after a frost. After straining the seeds and skins, they are suitable for cooking or making into a cranberry sauce. Although the odor persists while they are being cooked, it can be mitigated by adding lemon or orange. The odor does not transfer into jams and jellies, which require no additional pectin if the berries are hard and under-ripe (just turning red). Many Native American peoples considered them a prestigious food, making them valuable in trade and gift-giving. The berries were eaten raw, dried, or collected under-ripe and stored in water-filled cedar boxes to be eaten in the winter, usually with grease and other berries.

DESCRIPTION: This sprawling to erect deciduous shrub usually grows within arm's reach (2 m), though it can reach twice a person's height. The stems are usually no more than thumb-wide (2 cm) at the base and have smooth, dark gray bark that becomes rougher with age. The branches are oppositely paired, with younger branches and twigs being reddish. Twigs of the current season have four blunt edges rather than being perfectly round.

The **LEAVES** on the upper part of the shrub are oval-shaped with a pointed tip, have a rounded base, and may have three very shallow lobes. Lower leaves, however, are more distinctly 3-lobed. The leaf blade is palm-sized (10 cm), slightly longer than wide, and has edges that are bluntly to sharply toothed. The upper surface is dark green and short-hairy along the veins, while the underside paler and more hairy. The leaves are arranged opposite to each other, have leafstalks under 1 cm long, and turn bright, purplish red in fall.

In the early summer, creamy white **FLOWERS** with a musky odor emerge at the branch tips. The flowers are creamy white in front, pink behind, and arranged in compact, umbrella-like clusters (cymes) that are up to half a finger in diameter (5 cm) and contain 3–30 flowers. Each flower is roughly pea-sized (4–7 mm) and has five petals that are fused into a cup at the base, spreading out and surrounding five short, antenna-like stamens. In the mid to late summer, clusters of initially yellow **BERRIES** (actually drupes) ripen to orange to red. The smooth, shiny berries have a tough skin and juicy, acidic taste. Each berry is oval-shaped, about 1 cm across, and contains a single, flat stone that is hard and whitish.

HABITAT: This common native shrub grows from lowland to montane zones. In Alberta it occurs throughout the province, diminishing south of the line between Lloydminster and Calgary. It can be found in moist woods, thickets, mountain slopes, and along streams, lakes and bogs.

Highbush Cranberry

syn. Pembina

- berries have a tart, acidic taste.
- berry is about 1 cm wide.
- shrub can exceed twice a person's height.

WARNING: The raw berries should be eaten in moderation to avoid stomach upset. Spit out the seeds and the tough skin.

EATING: The raw berries are juicy, musky-smelling, and very tart, though their flavor improves after a frost. After straining the seeds and skins, they are suitable for cooking or making into a sauce. Although the odor persists while they are being cooked, it can be mitigated by adding lemon or orange. The odor does not transfer into jams and jellies, which require no additional pectin if the berries are hard and under-ripe (just turning red). Many Native American peoples considered them a prestigious food, making them valuable in trade and gift-giving. The berries were eaten raw, dried, or collected under-ripe and stored in water-filled cedar boxes to be eaten in the winter, usually with grease and other berries.

DESCRIPTION: This sprawling to erect deciduous shrub usually grows within arm's reach (2 m), though it can reach twice a person's height. The stems are usually no more than thumb-wide (2 cm) at the base and have smooth, dark gray bark that becomes rougher with age. The branches are oppositely paired, with younger branches and twigs being reddish. Twigs of the current season have four blunt edges rather than being perfectly round.

The **LEAVES** on the upper part of the shrub are oval-shaped with a pointed tip, have a rounded base, and may have three very shallow lobes. Lower leaves, however, are more distinctly 3-lobed. The leaf blade is palm-sized (10 cm), slightly longer than wide, and has edges that are bluntly to sharply toothed. The upper surface is dark green and short-hairy along the veins, while the underside paler and more hairy. The leaves are oppositely arranged, have leafstalks under 1 cm long, and turn bright, purplish red in fall.

In the early summer, creamy white, musky **FLOWERS** emerge at the branch tips. The flowers are pink behind, and arranged in compact, umbrella-like clusters (cymes). The clusters are up to half a finger in diameter (5 cm) and contain 3–30 flowers. Each flower is roughly pea-sized (4–7 mm) and has five petals that are fused into a cup at the base, spreading out and surrounding five short, antenna-like stamens. In the mid to late summer, clusters of initially yellow **BERRIES** (actually drupes) ripen to orange to red. The smooth, shiny berries have a tough skin and juicy, acidic taste. Each berry is oval-shaped, about 1 cm across, and contains a single, flat, hard, whitish stone.

HABITAT: This common native shrub grows from lowland to montane zones. In Alberta it occurs throughout the province, diminishing south of the line between Lloydminster and Calgary. It can be found in moist woods, thickets, mountain slopes, and along streams, lakes and bogs.

Russet Buffaloberry

syn. Canada Buffaloberry, Soapberry, Soopolallie

- ► berries are juicy with a bitter aftertaste.
- ► berry is pea-sized.
- ► shrub can exceed a person's height.

WARNING: The raw berries should not be consumed excessively, since their juice contains toxic saponins. Saponins are harmless in moderate quantity and are destroyed by cooking.

EATING: The raw berries are soft and juicy with a bitter aftertaste, becoming sweeter after a frost. Alaska natives traditionally pressed the berries into cakes, which were smoked and then eaten. A number of Native North American tribes collected the berries in large quantities by placing mats under the shrub and shaking the berries free. The smoked and dried berries were an important trade item and were typically used in strews, sauces (for buffalo meat), syrups and to make juice. Another popular practice was to make 'Indian ice cream'. To achieve this, raw berries were combined with an equal amount of water and beaten in a bowl free of any grease (and nowadays, plastic), which would prevent them from frothing. The foam was sweetened with berries or cooked bulbs and served as a treat during feasts.

DESCRIPTION: This erect, deciduous shrub typically grows as tall as a person (1.8 m), but can reach twice that height. The stems and spreading branches have shiny, reddish gray bark. The young bark is characteristically covered in small, rough, scales appearing as silvery or rusty brown dots. Older bark develops larger cracks. The slender, light brown twigs are arranged in pairs.

The **LEAVES** are elliptical or narrowly egg-shaped, rounded at both ends and somewhat leathery. The leaf blade is no more than a couple inches (5 cm) long and half as wide with smooth edges. The upper surface is shiny, light green and sparsely dotted with silvery, star-shaped hairs when young, turning a deeper green and becoming more densely dotted as the season progresses. The underside is densely covered with silvery star-shaped hairs and rusty brown scales. The leaves have short (3 mm) leaf stalks and are arranged directly across from each other on the branch.

Just before the leaves emerge in the spring, inconspicuous **FLOWERS** bloom, with male and female flowers appearing on separate plants. The flowers are arranged either singly or in clusters of several, emerging from where the leaves attach. They are a few millimeters across, greenish yellow on the front, brown on the back, and have four spreading, petal-like sepals that curve backwards. On male flowers, the sepals surround eight antenna-like stamens, whereas on female flowers they surround a single rod-like pistil. By the late summer, the female flowers develop into soft, juicy, orangey red **BERRIES** speckled with white dots. The oval-shaped berries are pea-sized (6–8 mm) and contain a single, flat seed. They are soapy when crushed and leave a bitter aftertaste.

HABITAT: This common native plant grows from prairie to subalpine elevations. In Alberta it occurs throughout the province, diminishing south of the line between Lloydminster and Calgary. It can be found in the understory of open conifer forests, on slopes, and forming dense thickets by rivers or in wet valley bottoms. It also thrives on rocky, sandy, or poor, gravelly soil.

Silver Buffaloberry

- berries are juicy with a bitter aftertaste.
- berry is pea-sized.
- thorny shrub is as tall as a one story house.

WARNING: The raw berries should not be consumed excessively. Their juice contains toxic saponins, which are harmless in moderate quantity and destroyed by cooking.

EATING: The raw berries are soft and juicy with flavor that is initially sweet but has a bitter aftertaste. Collecting the berries can be challenging, since the shrub has numerous thorns and the berries are often out of reach. The traditional technique of Native Americans was to place a mat beneath the shrub and shake the berries free. The berries were then sifted from leaves and other debris by rolling them in a container. After a frost, the berries are dislodged more easily and have an improved flavor. Smoked and dried berries were an important trade item and were typically used in stews, sauces (for buffalo meat), syrup, and juice. To make 'Indian ice cream', raw berries were combined with an equal amount of water and beaten in a bowl free of any grease (and nowadays, plastic), which would prevent them from frothing. The foam was sweetened with berries or cooked bulbs and served as a treat during feasts.

DESCRIPTION: This shrub or small tree can grow as tall as a one story house (6 m), often forming massive thickets. The main stems can become quite stout, and are covered in a thin, smooth bark that is light gray-brown. With age, the bark becomes darker and forms shallow furrows with flat-topped ridges, exfoliating in long strips. The stems are loosely branched, forming a rounded canopy that is about as wide as it is tall. The branches are oppositely arranged and the older twigs often terminate in stout thorns that can be a couple inches (5 cm) long. Younger twigs are dotted with flaky silvery scales.

The **LEAVES** are narrowly elliptical, tapering at the base, rounded at the end, and somewhat leathery. The leaf blade is no more than a couple inches (5 cm) long and about a quarter as wide, with smooth edges. The upper surface is green and silver-speckled from the presence of fine hairs, with only the mid vein being prominently visible. The underside is even more silvery, especially when young. The leaves are arranged directly across from each other on the branch, not appearing until several weeks after the plant blooms in the late spring.

The tiny, white to yellowish **FLOWERS** cluster along the stems and branches, with male and female flowers occurring on separate plants. The male flower is several millimeters wide and has four spreading, petal-like sepals that bend backwards when fully open, surrounding eight antenna-like stamens. The female flower is twice as large, with petals surrounding a single rod-like pistil capped with a bulbous stigma. By late summer, the female flowers have developed into soft, juicy, orangey red **BERRIES** speckled with white dots. The oval-shaped berries are about pea-sized (6–8 mm) and contain a single, flat seed. They are soapy when crushed and leave a bitter aftertaste.

HABITAT: This native plant grows in lowland elevations. In Alberta, it occurs in the southeast quadrant of the province roughly bounded by Calgary. It can be found in open forests and exposed hillsides, preferring moist but not shady areas near rivers, streams, lakes, and ponds.

33

Prickly Rose

syn. Arctic Rose, Bristly Rose

- ▶ hips are bland to sweetish
- ▶ hip is no wider than a finger.
- ▶ prickly shrub grows to chest height.

EATING: The berry-like hips have a thin flesh that is high in vitamin C and ranges from insipid to sweetish, improving after a hard frost. The flesh encases the seeds, which should not be consumed unless the hairs are first removed. Once the skin and seeds have been removed, the pulp is suitable for jams, jellies, marmelades, or syrup. Whole hips can be used to make a tea by crushing, boiling, and then straining them. They can also be dried and ground into a powder for use in cooking. Immature, green hips can be peeled and cooked, and both the flower petals and the tender, young spring shoots of the plant are edible raw. A number of Native American peoples, including the Thompson Indians of British Columbia ate the outer rind of the hips to a limited degree. The leaves and young twigs can be used to make a tea.

DESCRIPTION: This multi-stemmed, deciduous shrub rarely exceeds chest height (1.2 m). It has a straggling to erect form and may form thickets. The stout, woody stem are reddish or grayish brown and up to ½ cm wide. They have straight, slender, tan prickles that are under 1 cm long.

The **LEAVES** are compound, consisting of 5–7 leaflets that are arranged directly across from each other on short (1–2 mm) stalks, with a single terminating leaflet. The leaflets have an elliptical or inverted egg-shape and are rounded at both the base and the tip. The blade of the leaflet is no more than a couple inches (5 cm) long and is more than half as wide. It is often folded along the midrib and may have wavy edges that are coarsely and irregularly toothed. The upper surface is hairless and pale green, while the underside is slightly hairy. The compound leaves are as long as a pen (14 cm) and have downy leafstalks about 2 cm long. They are alternately arranged.

By the midsummer, fragrant, pink, saucer-shaped **FLOWERS** emerge singly or sometimes in clusters of 2–3 from short side-branches. The flower is wrist-wide (5–7 cm) and has five roundish, spreading petals that are lightly veined and often slightly notched at the tip. The petals surround numerous yellow, antenna-like stamens that are under 1 cm long. Immediately below the petals are five, narrow, leaf-like sepals, each a few centimeters long. In the fall, the flowers develop into smooth, fleshy, berry-like **HIPS** that range from being spherical or pear shaped to egg-shaped. They are initially green, becoming orange-red when ripe and persisting on the shrub into the winter. Each hip is no more than finger-wide (1.5 cm) and contains 10–30 stiffly hairy achenes (encased, dry seeds) that are each several millimeters long. The hip terminates with the dried, red sepals.

HABITAT: This common, native shrub grows from lowland to subalpine elevations. It occurs in the western half of Alberta, diminishing north of High Level. It also occurs in the eastern half, diminishing south of Edmonton. It can be found in open canopy forests, forest clearings, thickets, and on rocky bluffs. It also occurs along sandy shores, streams, swamps and roadsides.

Prairie Rose
syn. Wild Prairie Rose

- ▶ hips are bland to sweetish
- ▶ hip is about 1 cm wide.
- ▶ prickly shrub grows to chest height.

EDIBILITY: The fruits, or "hips" have a thin layer of somewhat sweet tasting but dry flesh around the seeds. The seeds should not be eaten unless their hairs are first removed, otherwise they can irritate the mouth and digestive tract. The seeds are high in Vitamin E and can be ground and mixed with other flours. The hips themselves are high in Vitamin C and were used by Plains Native Americans, though often only as a starvation food. They were sometimes dried and cooked into soups and stews. Other parts of the plant are also edible. The peeled young shoots are edible raw, as are the petals of the flowers, which are used in jam-making. The roots, hips, flowers and stems can also be used to make a tea.

DESCRIPTION: The plant is a perennial, deciduous shrub that grows below knee-height (50 cm) and dies back to the base each autumn. The flexible, erect stems have a reddish brown bark that is brown and woody near the base, becoming reddish brown to greenish above and dusted with a whitish bloom. The stems branch occasionally and are densely covered in straight, weak, reddish thorns. The thorns are usually just a few millimeters long and are unequal in length.

The **LEAVES** are compound, consisting of 7–11 leaflet that are arranged directly across from each other along a green to reddish central stalk (rachis), except for the single end leaflet. Each leaflet is oval or an inverted egg shape, with a base that is rounded or narrowed and a tip that is bluntly rounded. The leaflet blade is no more than a couple inches (5 cm) long and is about three quarters as wide, with edges that are coarsely and sharply toothed. The upper surface lacks hairs, while the paler underside is finely short-hairy. The leaflets have virtually no stalks. The compound leaves are no longer than a pen (12 cm), over half as wide, and are alternately arranged.

In the summer, fragrant, pink (or rarely white), saucer-shaped **FLOWERS** briefly come into bloom. The flowers occur in clusters (corymbs) of 2–5 , or rarely alone, at the ends of branches or on short, lateral branchlets. Each flower is no longer than a pinky finger (3–6 cm) and has five broad petals that are an inverted egg shaped. The petals surround numerous yellowish, antenna-like stamens and styles. Immediately below the petals are five long-tapering, pointed green sepals that are about half as long as the petals. In the late summer and fall, the flowers develop into clusters of smooth, reddish purple fruits, or "**HIPS**". The hip is usually spherical but can be oval- or pear-shaped, no more than a couple centimeters long and about 1 cm wide. It has a thin outer layer of flesh that encases 15–30 brown seeds (achenes). The seeds are under ½ cm long and are covered in stiff, long hairs. The hip terminates with five long, brown, dried out sepals.

HABITAT: This native plant grows from prairie to montane elevations. It occurs throughout the southern half of Alberta and in a large pocket around Grande Prairie, diminishing at latitudes north of Edmonton and in the northern range of the Rocky Mountains. It can be found in open forests, grasslands, pastures, fields, and along roads and fencerows.

Skunkbush Sumac

syn. Sourberry, Squaw Bush,
Three-Leaf Sumac

▶ berries are very sour.

▶ berry is pea-sized.

▶ shrub grows within arm's reach.

EATING: The berries have a tart, sour taste and an aroma similar to limes, which comes from gallic and tannic acids. Although they are small and have little flesh, they can be collected in quantity. A number of Native American peoples utilized the berries for food, especially in the American Southwest. They were traditionally eaten fresh as appetizers or used as a lemony seasoning agent. They were also cooked with meat or dried and placed in sacks for storage. In general, they are not suitable for boiling in soups or stews, since they release their acids and make the water astringent. However, they can be made into a refreshing drink by soaking them in warm or cold water.

DESCRIPTION: This deciduous, thicket-forming shrub rarely grows higher than a man can reach (2.3 m) and is typically several times wider than it is tall. The upright, arching, woody stems branch irregularly into a dense, rounded, mound-like canopy. The common name "skunkbush" refers to the bitter medicinal odor that is emitted from the foliage, particularly when it is crushed. The bark of the stems and branches is smooth and grayish brown, and develops a number of shallow fissures with age. The gray to yellowish brown twigs are fuzzy, becoming smoother as they mature.

The **LEAVES** are compound, consisting of three stalkless leaflets that can be bright or dark green. Each leaflet is no longer than a pinky finger (6 cm), with the central leaflet being largest. The leaflet blade is variably shaped, ranging from roughly elliptical to egg-shaped. It tapers at the base and has a variable number of rounded lobes that are coarsely and bluntly toothed. The surface of young leaflets is fuzzy, becoming smooth and glossy in maturity. The compound leaves are alternately arranged and turn orangey to reddish purple in the fall.

In the early to late spring, dense spike-like clusters (panicles) of tiny, yellowish white **FLOWERS** come emerge at the branch tips, opening before the leaves. Each cluster is a couple centimeters long and is crowded with numerous flowers. The flower is a few millimeters wide and long, and has five fuzzy petals that surround five tiny, antenna-like stamens. In the late summer or early fall, the flowers develop into small clusters of fuzzy, sour **BERRIES** (actually drupes) that range in color from dark red to reddish orange and smell like limes. Each berry is pea-sized (5–7 mm), imperfectly spherical, covered in slightly sticky hairs, and contains a single, dark brown seed.

HABITAT: This native plant it occurs in southern areas of Alberta, at latitudes southwards of High River and eastwards of the Rocky Mountains. It grows in grassland and shrubland areas of the prairies and foothills, preferring dry, rocky soils.

Seaberry

syn. Sea Buckthorn, Sanddorn

▶ berries are strongly acidic.
▶ berry is under 1 cm long.
▶ spiny shrub is as tall as a 1-story house.

EATING: The berries have a strongly acidic taste which decreases with cooking. They are richer in vitamin C than lemons or oranges and also high in vitamin A. To preserve their full flavor and quality, they should be collected before a frost. Though they may be too acidic to enjoy raw, they are suitable for mixing with other fruits to make juices. In Germany and France, buckthorn is used commercially to make wines, juices, and jams. Buckthorn tea, which has its roots in India, is another popular use for the dried fruit after the seeds have been removed.

DESCRIPTION: This multi-stemmed, deciduous shrub or small tree typically grows as tall a one story house (6 m), often forming colonies. Though it is highly variable in both form and size, it often grows within a person's reach (2 m). The stiff, woody stems range from brownish green to dark brown and tend to be covered with silvery scales or star-shaped hairs when young. The many branches and stiff twigs are heavily armed with spines that can be as long as a pinky finger (2–6 cm).

The narrow **LEAVES** are as long as a pinky finger (6 cm) and less than 1 cm wide, narrowing slightly at the base and gradually tapering towards the pointed tip. The edges of the leaf blade are toothless and may be slightly curved or curled back. The upper surface is characteristically a pale, silvery green. The underside is brown- or yellow-tinted and densely covered with silvery white scales. The leaves have short stalks and are alternately arranged on the branch.

In the early spring, tiny, inconspicuous, yellowish-brown **FLOWERS** come into bloom. The flowers emerge about one week before the leaves develop, with male and female flowers occurring on separate plants. Both the male and female flowers are a few millimeters long and have only two petals (actually sepals). The male flowers are arranged in a spike-like cluster of 4–6 that is under 1 cm long, and the female flowers occur singly or in clusters (racemes) of several from where the emerging leaves attach. By the fall, the female flowers have developed into bright, berry-like **FRUITS** that range in color from orange to yellow and hang along the stems and branches. The fruit has a diversity of shapes, ranging from spherical to oval or egg shaped. Each fruit is under 1 cm long and has a strongly acidic, fleshy pulp that contains a single, brownish black, egg-shaped seed. The fruit persists on the shrub.

HABITAT: This relatively uncommon, non-native shrub has escaped from cultivation and become naturalized. In Alberta, it occurs in and around urban areas, including Edmonton and Calgary. It can be found colonizing open land and forming thickets in abandoned fields, dry river beds, and wasteland. In its native Europe, it is found in coastal areas, hence the common name "Seaberry."

Pin Cherry

syn. Fire Cherry, Bird Cherry, Red Cherry

► cherry is very tart, has a large, hard pit.
► cherry is pea-sized.
► tree can exceed height of a 2-story building.

WARNING: The cherry pits can be fatally poisonous to children if consumed in quantity. Symptoms of poisoning include decreased pulse, dilated pupils, shortness of breath and unconsciousness. The toxins are destroyed by cooking or drying.

EATING: The cherries are very tart and have large pits. Their flavor improves after cooking or drying, and they can be used to make a good jelly. Native American peoples ate the cherries fresh or dried them. The dried cherries were sometimes ground into a flour and used as a soup thickener. The Iroquois formed the raw or cooked cherries into cakes which were dried and stored for future use. The dried fruit was taken afield as a hunting food.

DESCRIPTION: This deciduous shrub or small tree typically reaches three times a person's height (5 m), but can grow higher than a two story building (8 m). The stems or trunk have a smooth, sometimes shiny, bronze-colored bark that is quite thin and peels away in horizontal strips. The bark is prominently covered in yellowish orange, raised, scab-like pockmarks (lenticels) that form long horizontal gashes. The ascending branches spread into a canopy that is somewhat narrower than wide on mature trees. The twigs are light red, becoming duller as they mature.

The thin, light green **LEAVES** are narrowly elliptical, round to tapering at the base, and gradually tapering towards a long, pointed tip. The leaf blade is palm-sized in length (8–10 cm), up to a quarter as wide, and has edges that are finely serrated with blunt to sharp teeth. The upper surface and paler underside are smooth and hairless. The leaves rest on stems that are up to couple centimeters long. They are alternately arranged on the branch, turning bright orange to red in the fall.

In the late spring, almond-scented, white **FLOWERS** emerge near the branch tips in flat- or round-topped clusters (umbels or corymbs) of 5–7. Each flower is no more than finger-wide (10–15 mm) and has a stem up to an inch (2.5 cm) long. It has five spreading, egg-shaped petals that surround 15–30 antenna-like stamens. By midsummer, the flowers have developed into clusters of bright red **CHERRIES** that are very sour. Each cherry is spherical, about pea-sized (4–8 mm), and has a fleshy pulp that contains a single, large, pointed, seed.

HABITAT: This native plant grows from prairie to montane elevations. It occurs throughout Alberta, except in the northern range of the Rockies, the northwest quadrant of the province bounded by Fort McMurray, and the southeast quadrant of the province bounded by Red Deer. It can be found in dry to moist, open canopy forests, clearings, and thickets. It also occurs on rocky slopes, hillsides, and near streams and rivers, faring poorly in the shade.

Chokecherry

- cherries are very tart.
- cherry is about 1 cm wide.
- tree can exceed 3-story building.

WARNING: The hard pits of the cherries are poisonous.

EATING: The cherries are edible raw but can be extremely tart. After turning dark they are less astringent. Cooking or drying improves the flavor and destroys the poisonous compounds in the pit. The cherries are suitable for jams, jellies, syrups, wines, pies, and other baked goods. They were an important traditional food for indigenous peoples, including the Blackfoot and Plains Cree, who used them in soups, stews, and mixed them with fat to make pemmican. Fresh cherries were mashed and formed into flat cakes that were dried for later use. Cooked or greased cherries were fire- or sun-dried with or without the pits. In British Columbia, the dried cherries were often eaten with salmon or salmon eggs, and sometimes ground into a flour.

DESCRIPTION: This deciduous, shrubby tree has one or more stems and typically reaches three times a person's height (5 m), though it can exceed the height of a 3-story building (10 m). If multistemmed, the many slender, erect stems meet at the base; otherwise, spreading branches arise from a main trunk that is rarely wider than an outstretched hand (20 cm). The smooth, reddish brown bark darkens and grays with age and has small, raised pockmarks (lenticels) that develop into horizontal fissures. Younger stems have thin layers of bark that peel and curl more readily. The slender twigs are light brown or gray, usually hairy, and when crushed release an unpleasant odor reminiscent of bitter almond.

The smooth, deep green **LEAVES** are elliptical to egg-shaped with a rounded base, ending with a sharp, abruptly pointed tip. The leaf blade is no more than palm-sized (3–10 cm) and has edges that are finely and regularly serrated with sharp teeth. The upper surface is hairless and the paler underside may be short-hairy. The leaves have short (5–15 mm), often reddish leaf stalks and are alternately arranged on the branch.

In the late spring or early summer, white **FLOWERS** appear in elongated, cylindrical clusters (racemes) of 5–35 at the ends of new, leafy shoots. Each flower is no more than finger-wide (10–15 mm) and has five saucer-shaped petals that surround about 20–25 antenna-like stamens. By the late summer, the flowers have developed into hanging clusters of sour, shiny **CHERRIES** that range from red to purplish black. The cherry is imperfectly spherical, about 1 cm wide and has a single large pit, which is poisonous.

HABITAT: This common native plant grows from plains to montane elevations. In Alberta, it occurs throughout the province, diminishing northwards of Grand Prairie and Ft. McMurray. It can be found in open woods, clearings, forest edges, thickets, prairies, and rocky outcrops. It also occurs along lake shores, riverbanks, and fence-rows.

Greene's Mountain Ash

syn. Cascade Mountain Ash,

▶ berries are extremely bitter.

▶ berry is under 1 cm wide.

▶ shrub can exceed twice a person's height.

WARNING: Fresh, raw berries contain hydrogen cyanide and can be toxic if eaten in large quantities.

EATING: The berry-like pomes have an unpleasantly bitter taste which improves after multiple freezings. The flavor is further improved if the berries are allowed to blett (begin to ferment) and are cooked, at which point they lose their toxicity. Early settlers used them for jams and jellies, and they are still used to make wine, ale, and liqueurs. Most Native American groups considered the berries inedible, but some ate them fresh or dried them before grinding them into a flour. They were also used to marinate marmot meat.

DESCRIPTION: The plant is a deciduous, multi-stemmed shrub typically growing to twice a person's height (4 m) and forming dense, clumpy thickets. Occasionally, it becomes a small tree reaching as high as a 1-story house (6 m). The trunks are about fist-wide (10 cm) and are highly branched. The bark is smooth and shiny gray with a greenish or reddish tint. The slender twigs are olive green, have white hairs, and are characteristically slightly sticky with resin

The **LEAVES** are compound, consisting of 9–13 leaflets arranged directly across from each other in pairs, except for the single end leaflet. Each leaflet is long and narrow with a rounded bottom, tapering to a sharply pointed tip and lacking a leafstalk. The leaflet blade is no longer than a pinky finger (6 cm), about a third as wide, and has sharply toothed edges. The upper surface is a shiny, dark green and the underside is paler. The compound leaves grow to hand-size (10–20 cm) in length and are alternately arranged.

By the early summer, fragrant, creamy white **FLOWERS** appear in mostly-upright, umbrella-like clusters (cymes). Each cluster is highly branched and consists of 70–200 saucer-shaped flowers with white-hairy flower stalks. The flower is about 1 cm wide and has five nearly round petals that surround 15–20 antenna-like stamens. In the late summer, the flowers develop into dense clusters of up to 25 glossy, orange **BERRIES** (actually small apples, or "pomes") that have an bitter taste. Each berry is roughly spherical, under 1 cm wide, and has a fleshy pulp that contains several flattened, red-brown seeds, each about 4 mm long. The berries persist on the branch into the winter.

HABITAT: This common native plant grows from lowland to montane elevations. In Alberta, it occurs across western and central Alberta, diminishing eastwards of Edmonton and northwards of Lesser Slave Lake. In the Rocky Mountains and foothills it extends southwards into areas around Banff. It can be found in moist, open forests, forest edges, clearings, and along streams. At higher elevations, it occurs on rocky hillsides and in avalanche chutes.

Sitka Mountain Ash

syn. Western Mountain Ash

- ▶ berries are extremely bitter.
- ▶ berry is about 1 cm across.
- ▶ bush grows to twice a person's height.

WARNING: Fresh, raw berries contain hydrogen cyanide and can be toxic if eaten in large quantities.

EATING: The berry-like pomes are very bitter, but are high in carbohydrates and vitamin C. They are suitable for use in jams, jellies and wines, and improve with flavor after several frosts or after bletting (beginning to ferment), at which point they also lose their toxicity. They have been used occassionally for food by Native American groups, such as the Haida, but were not favored. The berries were either dried and ground into flour, boiled and eaten, cooked into soups, or used to marinate marmot meat.

DESCRIPTION: The plant is an erect, deciduous shrub or small, multi-stemmed tree whose size is highly variable, but rarely surpasses twice a person's height (4 m). Smaller forms tend to occur on more rocky or alpine sites. The stems have a thin bark that is gray and brownish or greenish tinged. The bark is smooth when young, sometimes becoming finely textured with age. The stems branch sparingly into a rounded crown. Young branches and twigs are olive-green. The new twigs are covered with fine, rusty hairs, but are characteristically not sticky from resin.

The **LEAVES** are compound, consisting of 7–11 leaflets that are arranged directly across from each other in pairs, except for the single end leaflet. Each leaflet is elliptical, has a rounded base, a bluntly rounded end, and no leafstalk. The leaflet blade is no longer than a pinky finger (6 cm) and is about a third as wide, with edges that are roundly or sharply toothed only on the top half of the leaflet. The upper surface is blue-green and the paler underside may have rust-colored hairs. The compound leaves are fist-size to hand-size (10–20 cm) in length and are alternately arranged on the branch, turning yellow, orange and red in the fall.

After the leaves are fully grown in the late spring or early summer, creamy white, fragrant **FLOWERS** emerge in dense, umbrella-like clusters (cymes) at the ends of branches. The branching cluster is no more than fist-wide (10 cm) and consists of 15–80 flowers. Each flower is under 1 cm wide and rests on a rusty-hairy flower stalk. The flower has five oval petals that surround 15–20 stamens. By the late summer, the flowers have developed into clusters of red **BERRIES** (actually small apples, or "pomes") that have a whitish, waxy coating and an extremely bitter taste. The berry is imperfectly spherical, about 1 cm across, and has a pulpy yellowish flesh that contains one or two elliptic, flattened, brown seeds, each a few millimeters long. The berries persist on the shrub into the winter.

HABITAT: This common native plant is scattered from foothill to alpine elevations. In Alberta, it occurs in the Rockies and foothills, diminishing northwards of Grande Prairie. It can be found in moist open forests, clearings, forest margins, thickets, rockslides, and in mountain meadows.

41

European Mountain Ash

syn. European Rowan

► berries are extremely bitter.
► berry is 1 cm across.
► tree grows as high as a 2–3 story building.

WARNING: The fresh, raw berries contain hydrogen cyanide and can be toxic if eaten in large quantities.

EATING: The raw berries have a strongly bitter, unpleasant taste and can cause vomiting if eaten raw. Even so, they are rich in vitamin C and are relatively easy to gather in quantity for making jams. In Scotland, the berries are used commercially to make jelly and in Switzerland to make juice. When dried, the berries can be ground and mixed into other flours for use in cooking. Since it is an introduced species, it was not traditionally utilized by Native Americans, though the berries of native Mountain Ash species were a (non-favored) food source.

DESCRIPTION: The plant is a deciduous tree typically growing as tall as a 2–3 story building (6–10 m), sometimes reaching twice that height. The crown is somewhat elliptical and about half as wide as it is tall, becoming broader with age. The trunk is rarely more than a foot (30 cm) across and has a smooth, silvery gray bark dotted with white pockmarks (lenticels). As it ages, the bark becomes grayish brown, rougher, and may become fissured with cracks and splits. The branches, which are spreading or ascending, are grayish with areas of new growth being green and often hairy. Older twigs are grayish brown and hairless,

The **LEAVES** are compound, consisting of 13–15 leaflets that are arranged directly across from each other on a central stalk (rachis), except for the single end leaflet. Each leaflet is narrowly elliptical, rounded at the base, and ends with a sharp or bluntly pointed tip. The blade of the leaflet is as long as a pinky finger (6 cm) and about a third as wide, with edges that are coarsely saw-toothed almost to the base. The smooth upper surface is light green and the paler underside is smooth or somewhat hairy, particularly on the veins. The leaflets have virtually no stalks and the compound leaves are alternately arranged.

In the late spring or early summer, mildly fragrant, creamy white **FLOWERS** appear in flat-topped clusters (panicles) that have light green, hairy stalks. The clusters are about fist-wide (10 cm) and consist of 75–250 flowers. The flower is about 1 cm wide and has five spreading petals that surround 15–20 white, antenna-like stamens. In the late summer, the flowers develop into clusters of **BERRIES** (actually "pomes") that are initially green, maturing to deep orange. Each berry is spherical or slightly depressed, 1 cm across, and has a bitter pulp with two seeds (rarely up to eight).

HABITAT: This introduced Eurasian species is a common ornamental landscape tree. Though rarely escaped from urban and cultivated areas, it is sometimes found in open forests, fields, near dwellings and by roadsides.

Red Elderberry

syn. Red Elder, Pacific Red Elderberry

▶ berries are unpalatable when raw.

▶ berry is no more than pea-sized.

▶ shrub grows as tall as a single story house.

WARNING: The raw berries are mildly toxic. They may cause diarrhea and nausea, particularly if eaten before fully ripe.

EATING: The raw berries are unpleasantly sour but improve after cooking or drying. After the seeds have been removed, the pulp is suitable for cooking into jellies and pies. Native Americans collected and used the berries extensively, sometimes cooking them into sauces. Some groups pit-cooked or steamed the berries on rocks before drying them for storage. The Nitinaht Indians pounded and dried the berries and later rehydrated them, adding sugar to make a jam-like food. The flowers are edible raw.

DESCRIPTION: This deciduous shrub or small tree grows as tall as a single story house (6 m) and has a clumpy form, sometimes growing in scattered patches. It has one trunk or several clustered stems that are erect and moderately branched. The smooth, dark, reddish brown bark is dotted with raised, oval pockmarks (lenticels) that are a couple millimeters long. The branches are typically arranged across from each other. Young branches are smooth, pale green or red-tinged, with new twigs being purplish and finely hairy. When crushed, the branches, twigs and leaves emit a characteristically rank odor.

The **LEAVES** are compound, consisting of 3–9 leaflets arranged directly across from each other on a central stalk (rachis), except for the end leaflet. Each leaflet is narrowly elliptical with an abruptly pointed tip and tapering base. The blade of the leaflet is up to half a foot long (4–16 cm) and between a third to half as wide, with edges that are irregularly and sharply toothed. The upper surface is smooth and dark green. The pale green underside may be lightly hairy, particularly along the central vein. Each leaflet rests on a short, light green to purple stem. The compound leaves are about a hand-long (18 cm), equally wide, and are alternately arranged on young branches.

For about three weeks in the late spring or early summer, pyramidal clusters of numerous, strong-smelling, creamy white **FLOWERS** emerge at the ends of stem branches. The intricately branched clusters (panicles of cymules) are about as long as a finger (8 cm) and half as wide as they are long. Each flower is up to ½ cm wide and has five backwards-curving petals that fuse at their bases to form a short tube. The petals encircle five spreading, antenna-like stamens that alternate with the petals and are capped with pale yellow anthers. In the midsummer, the flowers develop into clusters of shiny, juicy **BERRIES** (actually drupes) that are typically bright red, though some varieties are whitish, yellow or purplish black. Each berry is approximately spherical, no more than pea-sized (4–7 mm), and contains 2–4 small stones.

HABITAT: This common, native plant occurs from lowland to alpine elevations. In Alberta, it occurs in the Rocky Mountains and foothills extending to Lesser Slave Lake. It can be found in a range of habitats, including woodlands, meadows, and along rivers and streams.

Black Hawthorn

syn. Douglas Thornapple

▶ apples have a pleasant to bitter flavor.
▶ apple is about 1 cm wide.
▶ thorny tree is as tall as a 3-story building.

WARNING: Thorn scratches to the eyes can result in blindness. Pregnant or nursing women, children, and heart patients should not consume the fruit, which can affect blood pressure and heart rate.

EATING: The tiny apples or "haws" are mealy, dry, seedy and have a flavor that ranges from pleasant to bitter. They contain high levels of pectin, and are suitable for jams, jellies and pies. Some Native American groups considered them to be of poor quality and likely to cause stomach pains. Other groups ate them fresh, sometimes with salmon roe, or boiled them for prolonged periods before mashing and storing them. In the winter, they would be eaten with Eulachon grease, bear fat or marmot fat to counteract the dryness.

DESCRIPTION: This deciduous shrub or tree rarely grows higher than a 3-story building (10 m) and often forms thickets. It has several stems, or a single trunk that branches just above the ground. The stems are covered in gray to brownish bark that can either be smooth or rough and scaly. The stout, spreading branches form a compact, rounded crown. The slender, hairless twigs are shiny, reddish, and have stout thorns that are straight or slightly curved and 1–3 cm long.

The egg- to fan-shaped **LEAVES** are dark green, often with 5–9 shallow, pointed lobes, a tapering base and a short-pointed tip. The leaf blade is rarely longer than a pinky finger (6 cm) and almost as wide as it is long, with irregular teeth along the top edge. The upper surface is nearly hairless and the underside is a paler green. The leaves are alternately arranged.

In late spring, flat-topped clusters of several to many **FLOWERS** emerge on long, slender stalks at the ends of branches or where the leaves attach. Each saucer-shaped flower is white with a greenish center and no more than finger-wide (15 mm). It has five white, round petals that surround ten (sometimes twenty) pink, antenna-like stamens. The flowers emit an unpleasant, decaying-fish odor, though they smell pleasantly balsamic when freshly open. In the late summer, the flowers develop into drooping clusters of smooth, round **FRUITS** or "haws" that resemble small apples and are purplish black when ripe. Each haw is nearly spherical and about 1 cm wide. It has light-yellow pulp and 2–5 hard nutlets that stick together in the center. The nutlets are rounded at the ends and pitted along their sides. The fruits wither rapidly after ripening.

HABITAT: This native tree grows from lowland to montane elevations. In Alberta, it occurs southwards of Medicine Hat. It can be found in the forest understory, forest edges, and in the open, including meadows, valleys, and flood plains. It also occurs along shorelines, streams, fence rows, roadsides and in ditches.

Black Crowberry

- ▶ berries have a bland to sweet taste.
- ▶ berry is under 1 cm across.
- ▶ creeping shrub reaches ankle-height.

EATING: The berries are juicy and have a taste that is bland to sweet, though eating the berries alone may cause constipation. Some find their flavor disagreeable, though it improves after a frost or with cooking. They are often mixed with other berries and are used to make pies, jams, and preserves. Because of their hardiness and abundance, the berries were an important food for Inuit peoples, who foraged for them even in the winter, digging them from under the snow. They were eaten alone, with grease, or were made into a jam-like dessert by combining them with other berries, sugar, fish broth and other fish parts (blood, liver, heart). They were also preserved in large numbers by drying, freezing, or placing them in seal skin pokes with seal oil. A tea was made from the roots, berries and stems of the plant.

DESCRIPTION: This low, creeping, evergreen shrub often grows to ankle height (10 cm), forming a ground-hugging shrub mat. In rare cases, it reaches 2–3 times that size. The tough stems and many trailing branches are reddish brown and densely or sparsely covered with tiny, white hairs, with older stems peeling. Young twigs are green to light yellowish brown, turning darker with age.

The needle-like **LEAVES** are linear to narrowly elliptical, narrowing at the base and having blunt or pointy tips. The leaf is about ½ cm long and up to 1 mm wide with edges that are rolled under. The upper surface is smooth, while the underside is deeply grooved and has tiny hairs. The leaves, which lack leafstalks, are alternately arranged on the branch but are so closely crowded that they often appear as spreading sets (whorls) of four.

Between the late spring and midsummer, inconspicuous, dark purplish red **FLOWERS** briefly come into bloom. They appear either singly or as several, emerging from where the leaves attach. The flowers are up to a few millimeters across, have 0–3 petals and three petal-like sepals, with male and female flowers usually occurring on separate plants. On male flowers, the petals surround three markedly protruding, antenna-like stamens capped with egg-shaped anthers. On female flowers, the petals surround a single pistil. In the mid to late summer, the female flowers develop into clusters **BERRIES** (actually drupes) that are initially green, then red and finally become glossy black when ripe. The berries are spherical or slightly depressed, under 1 cm across, and have a juicy, bland to sweet pulp that contain 2–9 hard, light brown seeds. The berries persist on the branch into the winter.

HABITAT: This common circumpolar plant grows from lowland to alpine elevations. In Alberta, it occurs largely westwards of the line through Calgary, Edmonton and Ft. McMurray and also occurs at latitudes north of Ft. McMurray. It can be found in open, coniferous forests, sphagnum bogs and moors. It also occurs in dry areas with low organic content, including mountain summits, gravelly or rocky slopes, ridges, and windswept tundra.

Whortleberry

syn. **Common Bilberry,
Blue Whortleberry, European Blueberry.**

▶ berries are juicy, sweetish, slightly acidic.
▶ berry is under 1 cm wide.
▶ shrub grows shin-high.

WARNING: Because the berries have a high tannin content, consuming them over prolonged periods or in high doses can result in digestive disorders. They should not be consumed by pregnant women or patients who are undergoing anti-coagulation therapy.

EATING: The berries are juicy and slightly acidic, with a sweetish flavor. Their seeds are small, making them a good candidate for jams, and they are also used in jellies, preserves, pies and other baked goods. Though they are somewhat difficult to collect in large quantities, the berries were traditionally an important food for a number of Native American people, including the Thompson Indians of British Columbia and the Salishan Tribes. They were also collected by indigenous peoples in northern Europe and Siberia. The berries were commonly eaten fresh or dried for later use. The dried leaves can also be used to make a tea.

DESCRIPTION: The plant is a multi-stemmed, deciduous shrub that typically grows to shin-height (30 cm), forming open colonies. The stems and many slender branches are green to brownish, but may become red- or orange-tinged from the sun. The spreading branches and twigs are distinctly three-angled rather than perfectly round and the new twigs are finely hairy.

The **LEAVES** are elliptical to egg-shaped, tapered or rounded at the base, and end with a blunt or pointy tip. The leaf blade is about an inch long (2.5 cm) with edges that are finely and sharply toothed. The upper surface is light green and hairless and the underside is strongly veiny with a prominent midrib. The leaves are alternately arranged on the branch, turning brown, red, or yellow in the fall.

In the late spring and early summer, nodding, solitary **FLOWERS** ranging from reddish to creamy pink emerge from where the leaves attach. The waxy flowers are pea-sized (5–7 mm) and have five lobes that form an urn- or bell-shape. Within are 8–10 antenna-like stamens capped with yellowish brown anthers and a longer, white, rod-like pistil that may protrude. Between the midsummer and fall, the flowers develop into solitary **BERRIES** that range in color from dark purple or blue-black to (less commonly) dark red, and are often dusted with a whitish bloom. The berry is under 1 cm across and has a pulp that is characteristically purplish rather than white. It has a slightly acidic, sweetish taste and contains up to 40 tiny seeds. The berry terminates with a crown around a central depression.

HABITAT: This common plant occurs in montane elevations. In Alberta, it occurs in the southern range of the Rocky Mountains, where it can be found in the understory of open, coniferous forests, on hillsides and in moraines.

Thinleaf Huckleberry

syn. Big/Tall Huckleberry,
Square-twig Blueberry

▶ berries are slightly acidic and sweet.
▶ berry is up to 1 cm wide.
▶ shrub can reach chest height.

EATING: The berries are sweet and rather acidic, but have a pleasant flavor and are a good source of vitamin C. They stand out among huckleberries for their relatively large size and pleasant flavor, which make them popular for use in jams and jellies. The berry was an important food for many Native American groups. They were often sun dried for storage and later boiled and eaten, sometimes by cooking them with roots in a soup. The fresh berries were eaten raw or mashed into cakes which were dried for winter storage and later reconstituted in water. The Kwakwaka'wakw of British Columbia would cook them with salmon spawn.

DESCRIPTION: The plant is a deciduous shrub that can reach chest-height (1.5 m), often growing in clumps of several to many. The stems are erect, smooth, densely branched and spreading, developing a gray and shredded bark with age. In younger plants, the branches and twigs are green or yellow- to red- tinged. The young branches are slightly angled rather than perfectly round.

The pale green **LEAVES** are elliptical to egg-shaped, have a tapered or rounded base, and taper towards a pointed tip. The leaf blade is characteristically thin, hence the common name. It is no more than a couple inches long (5 cm) and about half as wide, with edges that are finely and sharply toothed. The upper surface is smooth and the underside is a paler green. The leaves have short leafstalks and are alternately arranged on the branch, turning bright orange and red in the fall.

In mid to late spring, solitary, urn-shaped **FLOWERS** come into bloom, nodding from just above the leaf stalks. The flower is about ½ cm long and ranges in color from creamy or yellowish pink to bronze. Within the rather wide urn is a rod-like pistil and 8–10 antenna-like stamens capped with relatively large anthers. By the late summer, the flowers have developed into shiny, purplish black **BERRIES** that have a pleasant taste. Each berry is spherical and up to 1 cm wide.

HABITAT: This common native plant grows in wet or dry areas, especially in montane or subalpine elevations. In Alberta it occurs throughout the Rocky Mountains and the foothills extending to Lesser Slave Lake. It can be found in forest openings, woodland edges, and mountain slopes, often as a dominant understory component.

Oval-leaf Blueberry

syn. Oval-leaved Bilberry,
Early Blueberry

▶ berries have a good flavor.
▶ berry is up to 1 cm wide.
▶ shrub grows to chest height.

EATING: The mature berries are pleasantly tart and somewhat seedy. Though not as sweet as other species of blueberry, they are a good source of vitamin C and are one of the most commonly gathered species in northern coastal areas of Canada. A number of Native American groups traditionally collected the berries, eating them fresh or cooking them in stews and sauces. The berries were typically prepared for storage by spreading them on a mat near to a fire and drying them into raisins. They were also soaked, mashed up, and then either formed into thin cakes or poured into rectangular frames and left to dry. The Comox Indians mixed them with Red elderberries and Salal berries. The Hesquiat Indians ate the fresh berries with the oil of whale, seal, or sea lion. The dried leaves were smoked by the Thompson Indians as part of a mixed tobacco.

DESCRIPTION: This slender, erect, deciduous shrub rarely grows beyond chest height (1.5 m) and does not usually form large colonies. The stout stems have a golden brown to purplish brown bark that becomes darker and more grayish, flaking off with age. The spreading branches and slender twigs are conspicuously angled rather than being perfectly round. The twigs are yellowish green and hairless, turning reddish with exposure to the sun.

The **LEAVES** are elliptical to egg-shaped and bluntly rounded at both ends. The thin leaf blade is up to half a finger long (4 cm) and just over half as wide, with edges that are usually smooth but may be very slightly toothed below the middle. The upper surface is a light grayish or bluish green. The paler underside is hairless, except possibly along the midvein. The leaves have virtually no leaf stalks, and are alternately arranged in ranks on either side of the branch, with the blades forming a plane. They turn bright red in the fall.

In the late spring to early summer, solitary, pinkish **FLOWERS** come into bloom, hanging from where the still-unfolding leaves attach. The flowers are under 1 cm long and have five petals that are fused into an urn- or egg-shape that is broadest at the base. Within are ten antenna-like stamens capped with relatively large anthers. From summer to autumn, the flowers develop into blue **BERRIES** that are characteristically dusted with a grayish, powdery bloom. The berry is spherical to slightly flattened at the ends, up to 1 cm across, and has a pleasant tasting pulp that contains numerous tiny seeds. The berry terminates with a very low, circular crown.

HABITAT: This plant grows from lowland to subalpine elevations. It occurs throughout the northern range of the Rocky Mountains and across central Alberta. It can be found in moist to dry forests, clearings, and on the shady edges of bogs, swamps, ponds and streams.

Velvetleaf Blueberry

syn. Canadian/Sourtop Blueberry,
Velvetleaf Huckleberry

► berries are tartly sweet.
► berry is pea-sized.
► shrub grows to shin-height.

EATING: The berry is tartly sweet, has a pleasant flavor, and is rich in vitamin C. It is used both commercially and recreationally for jams, juices, wines, pies, and other baked goods. The flowers are edible raw and can be used in salads or preserves. The berries were utilized by a number of Native American peoples. The Woods Cree dried them in the sun and then boiled or pound them into pemmican. The leaves are suitable for making tea, but have high concentrations of tannins and should therefore be used in moderation.

DESCRIPTION: The plant is an upright, deciduous shrub that grows to upper shin level (40 cm) and forms colonies of dense thickets. The stem, which is only a couple millimeters thick, is greenish and hairy. With age, it darkens to reddish brown or black and may peel slightly. It has many ascending, spreading branches and greenish brown twigs that are covered in dense, stiff, white hairs.

The thin, bright green **LEAVES** are narrowly elliptic, rounded at the base, and taper to a blunt or sharp tip. The leaf blade is up to half a finger in length (4 cm) and is about half as wide as it is long, with smooth edges. The upper surface and pale green underside are both soft-velvety, more so on the underside. The leaves have virtually no leafstalks and are alternately arranged on the branch, turning reddish in the autumn.

In the early summer, greenish white (sometimes pink-tinged), cylindrical or bell-shaped **FLOWERS** come into bloom. The flowers appear either singly or in dense clusters (racemes) of 2–6 that occur at the branch tips and along the branch, hanging from where the leaves attach. Each flower is about ½ cm wide and slightly longer. It has five petals that are fused into a cylinder or bell. Within are ten antenna-like stamens that do not protrude and a single, green, rod-like pistil that protrudes slightly. The **BERRIES** are initially greenish white, then pinkish, and finally, in the late summer develop into bright blue berries dusted with a whitish bloom. Each berry is spherical, about pea-sized (5–8 mm), and has a pulpy, sweet-tasting flesh that contain 2–25 small, golden brown seeds. The berry often terminates with a crown.

HABITAT: This native plant occurs throughout the western half of the province, including the foothills but not extending into the Rocky Mountains. It also occurs in the eastern half of the province at latitudes north of Edmonton. It can be found in open coniferous forests, treeless slopes, and forest clearings with gravelly or sandy soil. It also grows in disturbed areas such as clear cuts and burned areas, where it is an early colonizer.

Bog Blueberry

syn. Bog/Northern Bilberry

- ► berries are sweet and tasty.
- ► berry is pea-sized.
- ► shrub grows to shin height.

WARNING: Consuming berries infected with a fungus common to the plant may cause headaches and be toxic in large quantities. Pregnant or nursing women should not consume them.

EATING: The berries are sweet and juicy with a pleasant flavor and are a fair source of vitamin C. They can be used for making jams, jellies, pies, and other baked goods. A number of Native American peoples traditionally gathered them for food. The berries were dried whole for storage or preserved by mixing them with oil. They were also boiled in water and spread to dry. The Inupiat Eskimos ate the fresh blueberries alone or combined with blackberries and blubber. The berry juice was made into a vinegar which they used to pickle meats and greens. The Nauriat Niginaqtuat made a dessert by mixing the berries with sugar and either seal oil or fresh fish eggs.

DESCRIPTION: This stout, deciduous shrub has a variable form. When ground hugging, it forms large, dense mats that are boot-high (15 cm) and spreads by growing roots from the prostrate stems. When semi-erect or erect, the plant is usually shin high (15–40 cm) and often forms large colonies. The bark is grayish brown to reddish brown, becoming finely shredded with age. The main stem has many short, strong, brownish branches. The smooth, zig-zagging twigs are initially yellowish green, become grayish brown as they mature.

The **LEAVES** are elliptical or an inverted egg-shape, with rounded tips and a narrowing base. The leaf blade is no more than a few centimeters long and has smooth edges that are slightly rolled under, forming a narrow rim. The upper surface is dull green and hairless. The grayer underside is also hairless and has distinct, pale, net-like veins. The leaves have virtually no stalks and are alternately arranged on the branch. They turn bright red in the fall.

In the mid-spring, nodding, urn-shaped **FLOWERS** ranging from white to pinkish come into bloom. The flowers appear singly or in clusters (racemes) of 2–4 on short stalks at the branch tips, which continue to grow past the flowers. Each flower has 4–5 fused petals forming a roughly pea-sized (5–7 mm) urn. Within the flower are 8–10 antenna-like stamens capped with yellow, awned anthers. In the late summer, the flowers develop into sweet, blue **BERRIES** that are covered with a thin, grayish coating. The berry is spherical, pea-sized (5–8 mm), and contains a white, pulpy flesh. It often terminates with a short, wick-like flower remnant.

HABITAT: The plant grows from lowland to alpine elevations. In Alberta, it occurs throughout the northern half of the province, extending southwards through the Rockies to areas around Jasper. It can be found in boggy areas, peat bogs, muskeg and tundra, often associated with Sphagnum moss. It also occurs on alpine slopes, along rocky or sandy lake shores and on river banks.

Dwarf Bilberry

syn. Dwarf Blueberry

- ▶ berries are sweet with a pleasant flavor.
- ▶ berry is pea-sized.
- ▶ shrub grows below mid-shin level.

EATING: The berries are palatable and sweet when mature and are a fair source of vitamin C. They can be used to make jams, jellies, preserves, pies, and other baked goods. A number of tribes, including Okanagan-Colville Indians gathered and dry the berries for storage. The berries were also boiled in water and spread to dry into cakes. In the winter, the cakes were reconstituted in warm water and used for cooking. The Gosiute Indians of Utah dried the leaves and used them as a tobacco. The leaves and dried berries can also be used to make a tea, though the leaves contain high levels of tannins and should be used in moderation.

DESCRIPTION: The plant is a multi-stemmed deciduous shrub with a variable form. It rarely grows beyond mid-shin level (30 cm) and typically forms colonies. The stems are yellowish green or reddish and are usually finely hairy, becoming grayish brown and shredded with age. The stems are round (not angled) in cross section and have many twiggy branches, which are yellowish green and nearly hairless. The stems form roots where they meet the ground, spreading to form a low, nearly continuous, matted growth.

The thin **LEAVES** are a narrow, inverted egg-shape. They are characteristically tapered at the base, widest above the middle, and taper to an pointed or blunt tip. The leaf blade is no more than half a pinky finger in length (3 cm) and is about a third as wide as it is long. It is often lined with fine teeth or notches along the edges from the tip to the middle. The upper surface is smooth and light green or red-tinged, while the underside is a paler green with pronounced net-veins. The leaves have short stalks and are alternately arranged on the branch.

In the late spring or early summer, nodding, urn-shaped **FLOWERS** ranging from white to pink-streaked hang from where the leaves attach. Each flower is about ½ cm long and has five petals that are fused into an urn-shape with a constricted neck. Within are 8–10 antenna-like stamens. By the late summer or early fall, the flowers develop into nearly-round, sweet, blue **BERRIES** dusted with a whitish bloom. The berries are spherical or slightly flattened, about pea-sized (5–8 mm), and have a juicy pulp. They are not usually produced in abundance.

HABITAT: This common plant grows from lowland to alpine elevations. It occurs throughout Alberta, diminishing at latitudes north of Fort McMurray and south of the line between Calgary and Lloydminster. It can be found on mossy forest floors in dry to moist coniferous forests, in mountain meadows, near rivers, and on the shores of ponds and bogs. It also occurs on mountain slopes, alpine tundra, and rocky or gravelly banks, often preferring depressions in the terrain where moisture and colder air collects.

North American Gooseberry

syn. Hairystem/Swamp Gooseberry,
Northern/Smooth Gooseberry

▶ berries are sweet and juicy.
▶ berry is under 1 cm wide.
▶ shrub grows to waist height.

EATING: The berries are juicy and have a sweet, pleasant taste. They can be eaten raw, dried, or cooked into jams, jellies, preserves, pies, or other baked goods. The limited records that exist for this species indicate that the berries were collected at least by the Klamath Indians of Oregon, who ate them fresh or dried them for storage.

DESCRIPTION: The plant is a multi-stemmed, deciduous shrub that rarely exceeds waist height (1 m). The stems range from erect to arching, with roots and new plantlets growing from where the stems reach back to the ground. They have a brownish gray bark and may have short thorns where the leaves attach. If present, the thorns are under 1 cm long and are single-, double-, or triple-spiked. Between the thorns there may be a scattering of prickles, particularly on new shoots. The branches are hairless and form a canopy that is more erect than spreading. They do not emit a foul odor when broken.

The thin **LEAVES** are roundish to diamond-shaped with a flat to abruptly tapered base and 5–7 well-defined, rather pointed lobes. The leaf blade is usually no more than an inch across (2.5 cm) and is slightly wider than it is long, with the edges of each lobe having rounded teeth. The upper surface is dark green, nearly hairless, and not dotted with glands. The paler underside is also glandless but more hairy. The leaves have hairy stalks up to half an inch long (13 mm) and are alternately arranged, occurring either singly or in small clusters (fascicles) of 2–3.

In the late spring or early summer, **FLOWERS** ranging from greenish to purple come into bloom, dangling singly or in clusters (corymbs) of 2–3. The flower is about half an inch long (13 mm), with a ½ cm long, hairless stalk attached to the green, cone-shaped base. It has five broadly oblong, petal-like sepals that are pale green and often purple-tinged at the edges. They bend backwards, and surround five white to purple-tinged petals that are inversely egg-shaped. The petals, in turn, surround five protruding, antenna-like stamens that are characteristically twice as long as the petals and capped with cream-colored, oval-shaped anthers. In the summer and fall, the flowers develop into small clusters of smooth-skinned **BERRIES** that are initially green with longitudinal stripes and become purplish to black when mature. The berry is spherical, under 1 cm wide, and contains a sweet, juicy pulp that has no odor.

HABITAT: This native plant occurs across central Alberta, diminishing at latitudes north of Fort McMurray and south of Red Deer. It grows in forested wetlands, bogs, swampy woods, by lakes and along roadsides, in shady and sunny areas.

Whitestem Gooseberry

- ▶ berries are palatable.
- ▶ berry is under 1 cm wide.
- ▶ thorny shrub grows in arm's reach.

EATING: The berries are palatable but tart if picked too early. Like other gooseberries, they can be collected early and left to ripen. They contain high levels of pectin, which makes them well-suited for making jams and jellies. The berries were collected and eaten by a number of Native American groups, including the Thompson Indians of British Columbia, who ate them raw or cooked. Gooseberries in general were traditionally eaten raw, used sauces, or cooked and then spread to dry into cakes.

DESCRIPTION: The plant is an erect to sprawling, deciduous shrub not exceeding arm's reach (2 m). The hairless, loosely-branched stems have a pale gray bark that flakes off, revealing a deep red undersurface. The stems have strong, 3-pronged spines where the leaves attach. The spines are either straight or slightly curved and are typically up to 1 cm in length. In addition to having spines, young stems may be sparsely covered in backwards-pointing bristles. The twigs are yellow and often long-arching.

The **LEAVES** have 3–5 lobes and are rounded or indented at the base. The lobes are coarsely sharp- or round-toothed and are deeply divided, extending about halfway into the blade. The blade is no more than finger-long (2–8 cm) from one side to the other, and is slightly wider than it is long. The upper and lower surfaces are smooth to sparsely hairy. The leafstalks are about as long as the blades and are characteristically covered in long, filament-like hairs on the lower part and bare on the upper part around the leaf base. The leaves are alternately arranged, occurring in clusters of several from short side-shoots.

In the spring, white, tubular to bell-shaped **FLOWERS** with purple margins appear either singly or in clusters (racemes) of 2–4, drooping from where the leaves attach. The flower is about 1 cm long with a slightly shorter flower stalk attached to the green, tubular to bell-shaped base. Attached to the base are five pale green, backwards-curving sepals that surround five white, egg-shaped petals. The petals are about half as long as the sepals and form a tube that surrounds five protruding, antenna-like stamens. The stamens are characteristically twice the length of the petals. By the late summer, smooth, reddish purple to black **BERRIES** emerge. The berries are spherical, under 1 cm long, and palatable. They terminate with the dried, brown remnant of the flower head.

HABITAT: This shrub is native to western North America and grows from lowland to subalpine elevations. In Alberta, it occurs in the southwestern range of the Rocky Mountains. It grows in mountain forests, woodlands, moist meadows, along streams, and on moist to dry stream banks.

Canadian Gooseberry

syn. Northern gooseberry

► berries are mildly sweet.
► berry can be finger-wide.
► thorny shrub grows to waist height.

EATING: The berries have a mildly sweet, pleasant flavor when ripe, but may cause stomach upset if eaten in quantity. Though the berries are tart when picked too early, they can be collected early and left to ripen. The berries contain high levels of pectin, making them a good choice for jams and jellies. The berries were traditionally eaten fresh, dried, or cooked. The Cheyenne Indians formed the dried fruit into small cakes, which were stored for winter. The leaves of the plant are also edible raw.

DESCRIPTION: This erect to sprawling, deciduous shrub has a variable form. It typically grows below waist height (1 m) and rarely exceeding chest level (1.5 m). The stems are loosely and irregularly branched and under 1 cm wide at the base. They have grayish brown bark that becomes more whitish with age and usually have triple-pronged spines. The spines are about 1 cm long and occur where the leaves or branches attach. Stiff, reddish bristles that are a couple millimeters long may also occur either sparsely or densely along the stem. The twigs are greenish tan and hairy when young.

The **LEAVES** have five lobes and a base that is flat or roundly-indented at the stem. The lobes are rounded and have large, round, teeth at the ends. The blade is up to half a finger long (4 cm) and is about equally wide. The upper surface is dull green and hairless or slightly hairy. The underside is hairier, especially around the prominent veins. The leaves rest on stalks that are almost as long as the blades. They are alternately arranged, occurring in clusters of 3–4 along the stem where short side-branchlets emerge.

In the late spring or early summer, white **FLOWERS** emerge singly or in clusters (racemes) of 2–3, drooping from where side-branchlets occur. The flower is less than 1 cm long. Its stalk is about half that length and is attached to the green, tubular base (hypanthium). From the base spread five oval-shaped, white sepals that surround five egg-shaped, erect, white petals. The petals align to form a tube that surrounds five antenna-like stamens, which are characteristically shorter than or equal to the petals in length. In the late summer, the flowers develop into smooth **BERRIES** that are initially green, becoming reddish or purplish black. The berry is spherical, up to finger-wide (15 mm), and has a palatable tasting pulp that contains 5–25 dark brown, 3-sided seeds. The berry terminates with the dried, brown remnant of the flower head.

HABITAT: This native plant grows from lowland to montane elevations throughout Alberta. It can be found in moist forests, clearings, thickets, rocky areas and on sandy shores and riverbanks.

Trailing Black Currant

syn. Spreading Currant

- ▶ berries have variable palatability.
- ▶ berry is up to 1 cm across.
- ▶ shrub is waist high when unsupported.

EATING: The berries are not very juicy or abundant and have a taste ranging from palatable to unpleasant. Their low water content makes them relatively easy to dry and they can be used to make jelly. A number of coastal aboriginal groups are known to have eaten them, typically as they were picked rather than collecting them in quantity. The Hesquiat Indians of Vancouver Island ate the berries raw or cooked them with oil or sugar.

DESCRIPTION: This erect or creeping deciduous shrub does not usually exceeding waist height (1 m) and typically grows in small, dense clumps. It can be somewhat vine-like, climbing as high as a single story house (6 m) when supported. The stems, which lack spines or prickles, are purplish red, developing a dark brown or gray bark that becomes fissured with age. The loosely branching stems support twigs that are yellow-brown and covered in finely fuzzy, short hairs.

The **LEAVES** have five deep, triangular lobes, each ending with a pointed tip. The base of the leaf is deeply indented at the stem. The thin leaf blade is rarely more than palm-width (7–10 cm) and is almost as long as it is wide, with edges that are bluntly and irregularly toothed. The upper surface is dark green and hairless, while the paler underside is sparsely hairy on the veins, with small yellow, glandular dots occurring near the base. The leaves are alternately arranged and rest on leafstalks that are almost as long as the blades. They emit a strong odor when crushed and turn orange in the fall.

As the leaves emerge in the spring, clusters (racemes) of red to purple, saucer-shaped **FLOWERS** come into bloom. The erect or leaning cluster is usually shorter than a leaf and contains 6–12 evenly spaced flowers on short (1 mm) stalks. Each flower is pea-sized (6–8 mm) and has five petal-like sepals that are inversely egg-shaped. The sepals range in color from pale green to red and curve back at the tips, forming a saucer. Within the saucer are five tiny (1 mm), red petals that are widely separated, as well as five red, antenna-like stamens capped with white anthers. Between midsummer and fall, the flowers develop into clusters of purplish black **BERRIES** that have a slightly hairy or bristly surface and are dusted with a whitish bloom. The berry is imperfectly spherical, up to 1 cm wide, and has an unpleasant-smelling pulp.

HABITAT: The plant grows from lowland to montane elevations. In Alberta, it occurs in the Rocky Mountains. It can be found in shady, wet forests, forest edges, avalanche tracks, logged areas, and by mountain roads. It also occurs by stream banks and often hangs down from rock faces and old stumps.

Northern Black Currant

syn. Hudson Bay Currant

▶ berries are juicy but not palatable.

▶ berry is up to 1 cm wide.

▶ shrub grows to chest height.

EATING: The berries are juicy with seeds that are dense in nutrients, but their extreme bitterness makes them more suitable for jams and jellies than eating raw. Several Native American groups, including the Ojibwa, dried the berries. The Coast Salish of Vancouver Island would boil and then dry them into rectangular cakes that were eaten in the winter. In Alaska the berries were sometimes eaten after mixing them with moose grease and dried whitefish eggs.

DESCRIPTION: The plant is an erect to leaning, deciduous shrub usually growing below chest height (1.5 m). It has an unpleasantly sweet, musky odor. The loosely branching, thornless stems are no wider than a pinky finger (12 mm) and have a light brown to reddish gray bark that is covered in shiny yellow glandular dots. The branches are alternately arranged. Newer twigs are tan in color.

The **LEAVES** have three or five triangular lobes with the middle lobe being the largest, and are deeply indented at the stem. The blade is usually less than palm-length (10 cm) and is slightly wider that it is long, with coarse, irregular teeth along the edges. The upper surface may be hairy or hairless. The paler underside is studded with yellow dots and is usually covered with soft, shaggy hairs, at least on the veins. The leafstalks are deeply grooved and are almost as long as the blade. The leaves are alternately arranged on short side-branchlets, occurring in clusters of 3–6.

In the late spring and early summer, fragrant white **FLOWERS** appear in spike-like clusters (racemes) of 6–12 among the leaf clusters. Each flower is under 1 cm across and has five petal-like sepals aligning to form a short bell that flares into a star with blunted tips. Between the sepals are five tiny, narrow, white petals and within the bell are five antenna-like stamens capped with white anthers. By the late summer, the flowers develop into juicy, somewhat shiny, black **BERRIES** that are speckled with yellow dots and lightly dusted with a whitish bloom. Each berry is spherical, up to 1 cm wide, and has a bitter-tasting pulp that contains 10–20 smooth, reddish brown seeds.

HABITAT: This common plant grows from lowland to subalpine elevations. It occurs throughout Alberta, except in the southeastern quadrant of the province roughly bounded by Red Deer. It can be found in moist to wet areas across the northern boreal forest, including on stream banks, in forested bogs, and on rocky slopes.

Prickly Currant

syn. Swamp/Black Gooseberry

- ▶ berries are juicy and bland.
- ▶ berry is usually under 1 cm long.
- ▶ prickly shrub is usually waist high.

WARNING: Eating the berries in quantity may result in diarrhea or stomach upset. In some individuals, contact with the spines causes an allergic reaction.

EATING: The berries are juicy, faintly tart and have a disagreeable odor when crushed. They are suitable for making jams and were traditionally used by a number of Native American peoples. The berries were commonly eaten off the bush, cooked into a sauce, or stored for winter either by drying them whole or boiling and drying the pulp into cakes.

DESCRIPTION: This deciduous shrub has a variable form and grows either alone or in thickets, usually below waist height (1 m). In sunny areas, the erect shrubs can reach twice that height, but in shady areas they are often reclining or even trailing. The stems are loosely branching and have smooth bark ranging from cinnamon to reddish brown. Spines up to 1 cm long occur at intervals along the stem where the leaves attach. They are also sparsely to densely covered in shorter, straight, golden prickles. The younger branches are more densely prickly.

The **LEAVES** have 3–5 deep lobes, somewhat resembling a maple leaf, and a base that is flat or indented at the stem. The leaf blade is wrist-wide (6 cm) and not quite as long as it is wide, with edges that are coarsely and bluntly toothed. The upper surface is hairless and dark green. The paler underside has short, soft hairs, especially along the veins, and may be spotted with yellow glandular dots. The leafstalks are almost as long as the blades. The leaves are alternately arranged on short side-branchlets, occurring singly or in clusters of 2–4.

In late spring or early summer, tiny, saucer-shaped **FLOWERS** ranging from yellowish to pinkish emerge in loose, drooping clusters (racemes) of 5–15. The flower is pea-sized (5–7 mm) and has five egg-shaped sepals that form a shallow saucer. Within are five, stubby, antenna-like stamens capped with yellow anthers. The stamens alternate with inconspicuous, widely separated petals. By late summer, the flowers have developed into shiny, nearly round, purplish black **BERRIES** covered with bristly, sticky hairs. The berry is imperfectly spherical, typically under 1 cm long, and has a juicy, pulp that ranges from tasteless to faintly tart. It falls from the stalk when ripe.

HABITAT: This common native plant grows from coastal to subalpine elevations. It occurs southwards of Lesser Slave Lake in the western half of Alberta. In the eastern half, it occurs northwards of Edmonton. It can be found in ravines, swamps, and near stream banks, often on rotten stumps. It also occurs on forested slopes, in avalanche tracks, and on subalpine ridges.

American Black Currant

syn. Wild/Eastern Black Currant

▶ berries have variable palatability.

▶ berry is about 1 cm wide.

▶ shrub grows as tall as a person.

EATING: The berries have a variable flavor ranging from pleasant to so musky that they are only suitable after cooking or for use in jams and jellies. The Ojibwe ate them raw or dried them for winter use, when they would be cooked with sweet corn. The Iroquois also dried the berries, either in the sun or by the fire. The raw or cooked berries were also mashed and formed into cakes that were dried and stored.

DESCRIPTION: This multi-stemmed, deciduous shrub has no spines and typically grows no taller than a person (1.8 m). The woody stems are erect to spreading or slightly arching and no more than 1 cm wide. They have a smooth, grayish brown bark often dotted with white pockmarks (lenticels), becoming reddish to black at the base, particularly on older plants. Raised, light brown ridges run lengthwise along the stems, making them angled rather than smoothly round. The shrub is moderately branched with new growth green and finely hairy, becoming grayish as it matures. The older branches are hairless and darker brown or reddish.

The **LEAVES** are somewhat maple-leaf shaped, with 3–5 well-defined lobes and a base that is flat, abruptly tapered, or shallowly indented at the stem. The leaf blade does not exceed palm-size (10 cm) and is about as wide as it is long, with edges that are coarsely and irregularly toothed. The upper surface is dark green and hairless, appearing slightly wrinkly due to the sunken veins. The underside is hairy at least on the raised veins and is characteristically dotted with golden yellow resin glands that may also appear on the upper surface. The leaves have grooved, hairy stalks that are equal to or shorter than the blades. They are alternately arranged, occurring in clusters of 3–6 on short side-branchlets that are under 1 cm long. The leaves turn red and gold in the fall.

In the late spring or early summer, creamy white to yellowish, bell-shaped **FLOWERS** appear in drooping clusters (racemes) of 5–15. The clusters are no more than finger-long (8 cm) and emerge from the short side-branchlets. Each flower is about 1 cm long and has five backwards-curving, petal-like sepals. The sepals are oblong with rounded ends, and encircle the petals, which are aligned to form a tube that projects past the sepals. Within are five yellowish green, antenna-like stamens. In the late summer, the flowers develop into drooping clusters of smooth **BERRIES** that are initially green, turning black when mature. The berry is spherical, about 1 cm wide, and contains 10–20 slightly flattened, tan seeds. The berry terminates with the dried flower remnant.

HABITAT: The shrub grows from lowland to montane elevations. In Alberta it occurs across the province, diminishing at latitudes north of Ft. McMurray and south of Red Deer. It can be found in moist, open canopy woodlands, ravines, wet meadows, and on rock outcrops. It also occurs in swamps, by shaded stream banks, and along roadsides.

Creeping Oregon-grape

syn. Creeping/Prostrate Barberry

- ▶ berries are very tart.
- ▶ berry reaches pinky-finger width.
- ▶ shrub grows to mid-shin level.

WARNING: The raw berries contain the alkaloids berberine and oxyacanthine, which are toxic in large amounts. They should not be consumed by pregnant women. The spines on the leaves can cause a skin rash in sensitive individuals.

EATING: When raw, these sour, seedy berries are edible in small amounts, but can be toxic in large quantities. Their flavor improves after freezing, which makes them sweeter and safe to eat, but also breaks down the pectins, which are beneficial for making jams and jellies. They are suitable for use in wines and pies, and are high enough in vitamin C that they have been used to treat scurvy. If crushed in water, they make a drink similar to grape juice. The berries can also be dried whole, though they are rather seedy. The Blackfoot would eat them in times of starvation.

DESCRIPTION: This erect or creeping, evergreen shrub rarely grows beyond mid-shin level (30 cm) and typically spreads along the ground. The woody stems branch infrequently and are green when young, becoming gray-brown to reddish with age. The inner bark and wood is yellowish.

The shrub has 2–8 holy-like **LEAVES**. Each leaf is compound, consisting of 3–7 leathery, dark green leaflets that are arranged across from each other, except for the end leaflet. Each leaflet is elliptic, rounded at both the base and tip, and has virtually no stalk. The leaflet blade is no more than finger-long (8 cm) and is over half as wide, with spiny teeth along the edges. The upper surface is glossy to dull green, and the underside is paler and somewhat waxy. The compound leaves are up to hand-long (13–18 cm) and are alternately arranged, turning bronze, purple, yellow and red in the fall.

In the late spring or early summer, bright yellow **FLOWERS** emerge in upright clusters at the tops of the stems. Each cluster can reach finger length (8 cm) and consists of 5–20 flowers. The flower is about 1 cm across and has six spreading, rounded, yellowish sepals that surround six rounded, bright yellow petals. The petals align to form a cup, within which are six antenna-like stamens. In the summer, the flowers develop into clusters of sour, purplish blue berries that are dusted in a waxy, whitish bloom. The **BERRIES** are spherical to egg-shaped, as wide as a pinky finger (12 mm), and contain 1–4 large seeds.

HABITAT: This plant is native to the Rocky Mountains and grows from lowland to montane elevations. In Alberta, it occurs in the extreme southwest range of the Rockies. It can be found on dry, rocky slopes and gravelly areas with partial shade. It also occurs in open forests, often in the decomposing needles under conifer stands.

Mountain Fly Honeysuckle

- berries are sweetly tart.
- berry is about 1 cm long.
- shrub grows waist high.

EATING: The fruits are mildly tart but have a pleasant, sweet taste that has been compared to raspberries and blueberries. They are not commonly gathered by berry pickers since the shrubs are scattered and have sparse yields, but they are suitable for making jams, jellies, and drinks. There are a number of growing programs attempting to create commercial cultivars of this little-known berry, which is sometimes classified as a subspecies of *Lonicera caerulea* and marketed as "honeyberry."

DESCRIPTION: This deciduous shrub has an erect to ascending form and grows to waist height (90 cm). The woody stems are typically no more than ½ cm wide and have a gray bark that peels in vertical strips. The stiffly ascending branches are reddish brown to gray. On older branches and stems, where the thin outer bark shreds away, a reddish brown under layer is exposed. The smooth twigs and young stems are pale greenish brown or pink tinged and finely hairy.

Depending on the plant, the **LEAVES** are either green or reddish in the spring, becoming green by the summer. They are narrowly oval-shaped and widest above the middle, with a rounded base and tip. The firm leaf blade is typically no longer than a pinky finger (6 cm) and just over half as wide, with edges that are smooth and somewhat hairy. The upper surface is hairless and the underside is paler and hairy. The leaves have stalks that are no more than a few millimeters long and are arranged in pairs across from each other.

From the late spring to mid-summer, tubular, pale yellow **FLOWERS** emerge in pairs, hanging on short stalks from where the leaves attach. The pair is joined together at the base, where a green, cup-like bract occurs. Each flower is no longer than finger width (1.5 cm) and has five petals with round ends. The petals form a narrow floral tube that surrounds five slightly protruding, antenna-like stamens and a single rod-like pistil that is somewhat longer. By late summer, the flowers have developed into elongated, juicy, blue **BERRIES** that are dusted in a powdery, white bloom. The berry is about 1 cm long and has a sweetly tart pulp that contains 7–20 tiny, smooth, flattened, oval seeds, each a couple millimeters long.

HABITAT: This native plant occurs sporadically from lowland to montane elevations. In Alberta, it occurs in the central and eastern parts of the province, diminishing at latitudes north of Ft. McMurray and south of Edmonton. It can be found in wet woods, swamps, bogs, and stream banks, often growing in peaty soil. It also occurs in low pastures and rocky soils.

Saskatoon Berry

syn. Saskatoon Serviceberry, Juneberry

▶ berries are juicy, pleasant.

▶ berry is about 1 cm wide.

▶ shrub is as tall as a single story house.

WARNING: The berries contain cyanide compounds that can be toxic in extreme quantities. The toxins are destroyed by cooking or drying.

EATING: The juicy but seedy berries have a pleasant flavor and are excellent for use in jams, jellies, pies, and other baked goods. They are used commercially to make sauces, syrups, alcoholic beverages, snacks, cereals, and trail mix. Traditionally, they were one of the most important berries for Native American peoples and were a common trade item. Some varieties of the berry were dried like raisins and used in soups and stews, while others would be cooked, mashed, and slowly fire-dried into large cakes that weighed up to 7 kg. The Thompson Indians used the berries as a sweetener or for marinating other foods, such as lichen or roots. They were also made into pemmican by combining them with meat and fat. The leaves can be dried as used as a tea.

DESCRIPTION: This erect, deciduous shrub or small tree typically grows as tall as a single story house (6 m), often forming dense thickets or growing in clusters. The smooth, slender stems have a thin, gray to reddish brown bark that becomes shallowly fissured with age. The loose, ascending branches and twigs are reddish brown, often hairy when young, and tend to be alternately arranged.

The **LEAVES** are elliptical to nearly circular and rounded at both ends, though young leaves can have pointed tips. The leaf blade is up to a couple inches long (5 cm) and almost as wide. It has toothed edges along the upper half and is folded along the midrib when young. The upper surface is green to blue-tinted, mostly hairless, and has 7–13 parallel veins that run at a wide angle from the midrib. The paler underside is hairier, especially along the midrib. The leaves have stems that are about half as long as the blade and are alternately arranged, often on short side twigs. They turn yellowish orange to dull red in the fall.

In the spring or early summer before the leaves expand, white **FLOWERS** emerge in drooping to erect, leafy clusters (racemes) of 3–20 at the ends of branches. The flower is about an inch wide (2.5 cm) with an inch-long flower stalk. It has five elongated petals that narrow towards the base. The petals surround 15–20 antenna-like stamens. In the early to midsummer, the flowers develop into clusters of **BERRIES** (actually pomes) that are initially dull red, becoming purplish black with a faint powdery bloom. The berry is spherical, about 1 cm wide and has a juicy, pleasant-tasting pulp that contains 2–5 small, reddish brown (rarely white) seeds.

HABITAT: This common native shrub grows from lowland to subalpine elevations throughout Alberta. It can be found in dry, open canopy forests, forest clearings, woodland edges, thickets, and on sunny hillsides or mountain slopes. It also occurs by streams and lakeshores.

Common Juniper

▶ berries are hard, mealy, astringent.

▶ berry is pea-sized.

▶ shrub usually grows below waist height.

WARNING: The berries act as an intestinal antiseptic and strong diuretic. Eating them in excessive quantities can cause renal damage or intestinal irritation. They should not be consumed by pregnant women or people with kidney problems.

EATING: The berries have a pitchy, astringent taste and resinous texture, and are not generally eaten raw. They are used commercially to make an extract used in the flavoring of gin and other alcoholic beverages (the word "gin" is derived from the French "genievre," referring to the Juniper berry). The dried berries are crushed and used to flavor meats, especially those of wild game. They can also be used as a pepper in soups, stews, sauces, or stuffings. In Germany, they are used to flavor sauerkraut and a type of jam called "Latwerge." In India, they are used in making curries. The seeds can be roasted and used as a coffee substitute and the leaves, stems and berries can be boiled to make a spicy tea whose flavor is reminiscent of gin.

DESCRIPTION: The plant is a multi-stemmed, evergreen shrub or less commonly a small tree. It is often less than waist high (1 m), and sprawls to create a dense, clumpy mat with a distinctive, pungent odor. As a tree, it has a column-like form, occasionally growing beyond a person's reach (2.2 m). The stems, which are usually hidden by foliage, have brown to gray, scaly bark that shreds off in thin strips. The many branches are reddish brown and usually arranged across from each other. They are inclined about 45 degrees from the ground and spread widely. The slender, smooth twigs are yellowish green when young and three-sided rather than being perfectly round.

The **LEAVES** are flatly needle shaped, stiff, and have sharp tips. They are about 1 cm long and arranged in sets (whorls) of three at a wide angle from the twig. The upper surface of each needle is whitish green and has a white channel running down its length, while the underside is a darker green. Male and female **CONES** appear on the branches of separate plants. The male cones are yellow, almost ½ cm long and a few millimeters wide, falling off in the spring. The female cones are initially green and take about a year and a half to ripen into hard, blue, mealy **"BERRIES."** They have a waxy, whitish coating and strong odor when crushed. Each berry is roughly spherical, pea-sized (6–8 mm), and contains several small seeds.

HABITAT: This native plant grows from lowland to alpine elevations. It occurs throughout the Rockies, extending into central areas as far east as Edmonton and Calgary. It also occurs in a large pocket around Grande Prairie and in the northeast corner of the province. It can be found in dry, open woods and in rocky, infertile soil, including exposed slopes, ridges and outcrops.

Rocky Mountain Juniper

- berries are astringent to sweetish.
- berry is pea-sized.
- shrub grows as tall as a 3–5 story building.

WARNING: The berries act as an intestinal antiseptic and strong diuretic. Eating them in excessive quantities can cause renal damage or intestinal irritation. They should not be consumed by pregnant women or people with kidney problems.

EATING: The berries are pitchy and resinous, ranging in taste from strongly astringent to sweetish. Though they are edible raw, they are typically dried, crushed, and used to flavor other foods. The berries were used by some tribes for food. They ate them raw, cooked them in stews, or ground the dried berries into a meal that was used for making mush or cakes. The roasted berry can be used as a coffee substitute.

DESCRIPTION: This plant has a variable form that is dependent on its growing conditions. It can be a sprawling evergreen shrub growing to waist height (1 m) or a roundly conical tree reaching as high as a 3–5 story building (9–15 m). The reddish brown to gray bark is smooth or flaky when young and exfoliates in thin strips when older. The trunk is densely branched to ground level, with branches inclined and spreading. Trees growing in the shade tend to have foliage with a drooping or weeping appearance. The young branches and twigs are 3- or 4- angled rather than round, and are obscured by a covering of short, scale-like needles that can give the impression of a braided cord.

The **LEAVES** lie flat against the twig in alternating pairs that slightly overlap. They have blunt tips, smooth edges, and are just a few millimeters long. Their color varies from green to blue-tinted, turning brown at the end of the season. On young seedlings, the leaves are longer (up to 1 cm) and more needle-like, arranged in sets (whorls) of three along the twigs.

In the spring, inconspicuous **CONES** just a few millimeters wide appear at the branch tips, with male and female cones appearing on separate plants. The male cones are yellowish brown and oblong. The female cones are greenish yellow, nearly spherical and consist of 3–8 scales. Over the course of about two years, the female cones become berry-like. The **BERRIES** are initially green, becoming blue with a waxy, whitish bloom when mature. They are imperfectly spherical, pea-sized (6–8 mm) and have a pungent-smelling pulp that contains up to a dozen small, round, brownish seeds. The berries persist on the shrub through the winter.

HABITAT: This native plant grows from lowland to montane elevations. In Alberta it occurs in the southern parts of the province, at latitudes south of Medicine Hat. It also extends northwards into the Rocky Mountains, diminishing north of Banff. It can be found in rocky or exposed sites, including on ridges, cliffs and foothills. It also occurs in dry, open terrain, such as prairie hillsides, fields and pastures.

Creeping Juniper

syn. Creeping Cedar

► berries are hard, mealy, astringent.
► berry is pea-sized
► shrub grows about a foot high.

WARNING: The berries act as an intestinal antiseptic and strong diuretic. Eating them in excessive quantities can cause renal damage or intestinal irritation. They should not be consumed by pregnant women or people with kidney problems.

EATING: The berries are hard, mealy, and astringent but high in vitamin C. As with other Juniper berries, their flavor improves after the second season and they can be used to flavor meats or dried and crushed into a spice. There is no record that the berries of this species were eaten by Native American groups, though the Ojibwa used the leaves from the branch tips of younger plants to make a tea.

DESCRIPTION: The plant is a creeping, multi-stemmed, evergreen shrub rarely growing higher than one foot (30 cm) and often forming a dense, flat, vegetative mat that covers several square meters or more. The stems are up to ½ cm thick and have a tan, scaly bark that becomes reddish brown and peels with age, though it is typically hidden by the foliage. The flexible, horizontal branches sprawl along the ground, forming roots. They have many short, erect, side-branches and twigs.

The twigs are densely covered in pointed, stalkless **LEAVES** that range from yellowish to bluish green. On young plants, the leaves are needle-like, spreading and just over ½ cm long at most. On mature plants the leaves are about 1½ mm long and are closely appressed to the twigs in an overlapping, scale-like fashion. They are arranged in opposite pairs or in sets (whorls) of three, sometimes turning purplish in the winter.

Male and female **CONES** appear on separate plants at the tips of first- and second-year branches. The yellowish brown male cones are yellow brown becoming purplish and occur at the branch tips. They are cylindrical in shape, almost ½ cm long and a few millimeters wide. The female cones are spherical and initially green, maturing in 15–20 months. In the fall, they develop into small clusters of hard, blue, mealy **"BERRIES"** that rest on short, backwards-curving stalks. The berries have a whitish coating and strong odor when crushed. Each berry is imperfectly spherical, pea-sized (6–8 mm), and contains 1–5 reddish brown, oval seeds.

HABITAT: This native shrub grows from lowland to montane elevations. In Alberta, it occurs at latitudes south of Edmonton, diminishing south of the line between Calgary and Lloydminster. It also occurs in a large pocket around High Level and the extreme northeast corner of the province. It can be found in dry, open woods, prairies, and fields. At higher elevations, it grows in dry, rocky or sandy soil on slopes and rocky outcrops.

Creeping Snowberry

syn. Moxie-Plum

▶ berries taste of wintergreen.

▶ berry is about pea-sized.

▶ leaves are edible.

▶ creeping shrub is ankle-high.

WARNING: The berries and other plant parts should not be consumed by those allergic to aspirin.

EATING: The berries contain oil of wintergreen, which gives them a mildly acidic, refreshing taste reminiscent of a Tic-Tac™. Their flavor improves after a freezing, and since they persist on the bush, can be collected during the winter or spring thaw. They can be used in making jams, sauces, pies and other baked goods, and are used commercially to flavor liqueurs. The fresh berries are sometimes used in salads, eaten with cream and sugar or collected as a trail-side nibble. The Algonquin of Quebec are known to have collected the berries for food. The leaves, which are edible raw or cooked, were used by the Chippewa and others to make a tea that was often sweetened with maple sugar.

DESCRIPTION: This delicate, ground-hugging, evergreen shrub rarely grows above ankle-height (10 cm), usually appearing as tufts or forming densely matted clumps. The slender, leafy, horizontal stems have stiff, straight brown hairs that lay flat. They usually grow as long as a hand (20 cm) or sometimes to twice that length, forming roots where they meet the ground. The stems are green when young, turning yellowish brown with age.

The small, firm **LEAVES** are elliptical, tapering at both ends and having a pointed tip. The leaf blade is about 1 cm long and has smooth edges that are slightly curled under. The upper surface is smooth and has an impressed midvein. The paler underside characteristically has coarse, reddish, bristly hairs. The leaves have virtually no leaf stalks and are alternately arranged on the stem.

In the late spring, solitary, bell-shaped **FLOWERS** ranging from white to pinkish come into bloom. Each flower hangs from a light green, curved flower stalk that attaches just above a leaf. The flower is about ½ cm long and has four spreading, petal-like sepals that surround four similar-looking petals. The petals are fused at their bases, forming a bell around 8–10 short (1 mm) antenna-like stamens. By late summer, the flowers develop into white, mealy **BERRIES** covered in minute bristly hairs. The berry is egg-shaped and up to 1 cm long, with a wintergreen-flavored pulp that contains two or more seeds. The berries persist on the plant into the winter.

HABITAT: This native plant often grows from montane to subalpine elevations. In Alberta, it occurs across the central province, diminishing at latitudes north of Ft. McMurray and south of Jasper. It also occurs throughout the Rocky Mountains and foothills. It can be found in damp forests, on stumps, mounds of moss, decaying logs, and in bogs.

Silverberry

syn. American Silverberry, Wolf Willow

► berries are dry and mealy.
► berry is about 1 cm long.
► shrub grows to twice a person's height.

EATING: The berries are dry and mealy. They are too astringent to be enjoyed when even slightly unripened, but their flavor improves after a frost or when frozen and they can be made into an excellent jam or jelly. The berries were widely used by Native American peoples, though most considered them famine food. The Blackfoot peeled the berries and ate them with grease or used them in soups. It was also common to cook the berries in grease, blood, or in the case of Alaska natives, to fry them in moose fat. The seeds are edible raw or cooked and were an important food for the Paiute.

DESCRIPTION: This single- or multi-stemmed, deciduous shrub grows to twice a person's height (3.5 m). It is about as wide as it is tall and forms dense thickets or loose colonies. The flexible stems are no more than finger-wide (1.5 cm) and have silvery brown, scaly bark which becomes darker and less silvery with age. The stems have branches that are alternately arranged and form a mounded, open crown. Rusty brown and silvery scales cover both the branches and twigs, which are greenish brown in areas of new growth.

The silvery **LEAVES** are elliptical to narrowly egg-shaped, widest near the middle or the end, and bluntly rounded or short-pointed at both ends. The leaf blade is no more than finger-long (8 cm) and is about half as wide, with edges that are smooth and often slightly wavy. The upper surface is characteristically densely dotted with tiny, silver scales. The paler underside has silvery or rusty brown scales. The leaves have stalks under ½ cm long and are alternately arranged on the twigs.

In the early summer, fragrant, yellow **FLOWERS** emerge in clusters (cymes) of 2–4, hanging on short flower stalks from where the leaves attach. The flower is about 1 cm wide and half again as long, with four rather thick, pointed petals (actually sepals). The petals are fused into a tube that flares out at the end and surrounds four antenna-like stamens. The tube is silvery on the outside, yellow within and on the face. By late summer, the flowers develop into egg-shaped, silvery **BERRIES** (actually drupes) that are about 1 cm long. The berry has a thick, papery outer layer and contains a dry, mealy, whitish green pulp with a single large seed that is narrow and hollow. The berries persist on the branch into the winter.

HABITAT: This native plant grows from lowland to montane elevations. In Alberta, it occurs throughout the southern half of the province and north of the line between High Level and Fort McMurray. It also occurs in a isolated pocket around Grande Prairie. It can be found at forest edges, in ravines and on prairie grasslands. It also grows on gravelly river banks and shorelines.

Red Osier Dogwood

syn. Red Twig Dogwood,
Western/Creek/American Dogwood

- ▶ berries are bitter and poor tasting.
- ▶ berry is pea-sized.
- ▶ shrub grows to twice a person's height.

WARNING: The berries can cause nausea and may be toxic if eaten in large quantities.

EATING: The berries are bitter and unpalatable, but were eaten by a number of Native American groups, including the Blackfoot, who ate them raw. The Okanagan-Colville Indians boiled them or mixed them with Saskatoon berries. Other groups pounded them with choke-cherries (including the seeds) or mashed them with sweeter berries, forming cakes which were dried for winter use.

DESCRIPTION: This deciduous, multi-stemmed shrub can reach twice a person's height (3.5 m), often forming dense, clumpy thickets. The slender, erect to leaning stems have a diameter no more than half a finger (4 cm) long. The shiny, reddish bark is dotted with small (2 mm), white, oval pockmarks (lenticels). With age, the stems become woody and the bark becomes grayish brown or greenish, developing cracks and splits. The branches are purple to red and contain a large, white pith. They are oppositely arranged, often occurring on the stem just above a white ring, with the lower branches forming roots where they meet the ground. Twigs of the current season are olive green and finely hairy.

The **LEAVES** are elliptical with a rounded base and pointed tip. The leaf blade is no longer than a pen (12 cm) and is about two thirds as wide as it is long, with smooth edges, near. The upper surface is smooth, hairless, and has 5–7 pairs of prominent, sunken veins that curve forward. The underside is paler and hairier. The leaves have stems up to an inch long (2.5 cm) and are arranged across from each other, turning purplish to red in the fall.

In the late spring or early summer, fragrant, creamy white **FLOWERS** emerge at the branch tips. The flowers are crowded into flat-topped clusters (cymes) of 17–130, with each cluster no more than a few inches wide (7.5 cm). Each flower is under 1 cm wide and has four narrow, pointed, spreading petals that are white or green-tinged. The petals surround four greenish, antenna-like stamens capped with yellow anthers. By the late summer or fall, the flowers develop into smooth, white or blue-tinged **BERRIES** (actually drupes) that occur in rounded clusters of 10–30. Each berry is imperfectly spherical, pea-sized (4–6 mm), and has a bitter, fleshy pulp containing a single, large, flattened stone that is grayish brown.

HABITAT: This native plant grows from lowland to montane elevations. It occurs throughout Alberta, diminishing southwards and eastwards of Drumheller. It can be found in wet forests, meadows, shrubby bogs, swamps, and near rivers or streams.

Plains Prickly-pear

▶ berries are slightly sweet.
▶ berry is about an inch long.
▶ young pads can be cooked.
▶ cactus grows to boot high.

WARNING: This cactus has small, barbed prickles that can be difficult to see, but easily become painfully embedded in the skin

EATING: The raw berries are edible once the spiny outer layer has been removed. They are somewhat sweet and are high in vitamin C. A number of Native American peoples traditionally collected them for food. The small bristles

were sometimes removed by rolling the berries in sand or by sweeping them with branches. After carefully removing any remaining bristles, the fruit was split open to remove the seeds, which could be dried and ground into a mush. The berry pulp was eaten fresh, used to thicken soups and stews, or dried for storage. The young pads of the cactus are also edible when cooked and have a cucumber-like taste. The juice can be used as an emergency water source.

DESCRIPTION: This ground-hugging cactus rarely grows beyond boot height (18 cm) and often forms clumpy mats about a meter wide. The grayish-green stems are typically horizontal and are divided into branching segments (or "pads"), which constitute the body of the cactus. Each segment is round to oval, up to half a foot (15 cm) long and several times longer than it is thick, giving it a distinctly flattened appearance. The segments are firmly attached to each other and are covered with rows of small bumps (areoles), with 4–14 occurring along each diagonal row.

At each areole (or sometimes only on those of the upper half), a cluster of 5–11 sharp, rigid **SPINES** spreads outwards. The spines are straight to slightly curved, rarely more than a couple inches (5 cm) long, and range from white to yellowish brown. The base of the spines is woolly-hairy, and hosts numerous smaller, yellow to reddish prickles that are about 1 cm long.

In the late spring or early summer, pale yellow **FLOWERS** sometimes emerge — either on the uppermost segment or a terminal branch segment. The flower is a couple inches (5 cm) wide and long. It has seven or more thin, spreading, waxy petals that are tapered at the base and rounded at the end. The petals surround numerous antenna-like stamens capped with yellow anthers. The flowers develop into **BERRIES** that are initially green to purplish, becoming tan and dry when ripe. The berry is pear- or barrel-shaped and about an inch (2.5 cm) long, with tiny spines emerging from the upper areoles. It contains several pea-sized (3–7 mm) seeds that are white and disc-shaped.

HABITAT: This common, native cactus grows from prairie to mid elevations. In Alberta, it occurs in the southeast quadrant of the province roughly bounded by Calgary. It can be found in grasslands, prairies, foothills, and on dry, exposed slopes. It may also occur in sparsely wooded areas and rocky terrain.

alkaloid: bitter tasting, natural bases containing nitrogen that are found in plants.

alternate: first on one side and then on the other in two ranks along an axis; not paired.

alpine: living or growing above the timber line.

anthers: the part of the stamen that contains pollen; usually borne on a stalk.

basal: located at the base of a plant or stem; especially arising directly from the root or rootstock or a root-like stem.

berry: a small fruit having any of various structures, e.g., simple (grape or blueberry) or aggregate (blackberry or raspberry).

bog: wet spongy ground of decomposing vegetation; has poorer drainage than a swamp.

bract: a modified leaf or leaf-like part just below and protecting an inflorescence.

bud: a swelling on a plant stem consisting of overlapping immature leaves or petals.

catkin: a cylindrical spikelike inflorescence.

compound leaf: a leaf composed of a number of leaflets on a common stalk.

cone: cone-shaped mass of ovule- or spore-bearing scales or bracts.

conifer: any gymnospermous tree or shrub bearing cones.

corymb: flat-topped or convex inflorescence in which the individual flower stalks grow upward from various points on the main stem to approximately the same height; outer flowers open first.

crown: the upper branches and leaves of a tree or other plant.

cyme: more or less flat-topped cluster of flowers in which the central or terminal flower opens first.

cymule: a small cyme, generally with few flowers.

deciduous: shedding foliage at the end of the growing season.

dermatitis: inflammation of the skin; skin becomes itchy and may develop blisters.

drupe: fleshy indehiscent fruit with a single seed (such as almond, peach, plum, cherry, elderberry, olive or jujube).

drupelet: a small part of an aggregate fruit that resembles a drupe.

elliptical: oval shaped.

evergreen: bearing foliage throughout the year.

foliage: leafage.

fruit: the ripened reproductive body of a seed plant.

grease: the oil extracted from the Eulachon fish and traditionally used in a manner similar to butter by coastal peoples.

haw: the fruit of a hawthorn tree.

herb/herbaceous: a plant lacking a permanent woody stem.

hip: the fruit of a rose plant.

leaflet: part of a compound leaf.

lenticel: one of many raised pores on the stems of woody plants that allow the interchange of gas between the atmosphere and the interior tissue.

lobe: a part into which a leaf is divided.

midrib, midvein: the vein in the center of a leaf.

montane: of or inhabiting mountainous regions.

moor: open land usually with peaty soil covered with heather and bracken and moss.

node: the small swelling that is the part of a plant stem from which one or more leaves emerge.

nutlet: a small nut.

opposite: growing in pairs on either side of a stem.

outcrop: the part of a rock formation that appears above the surface of the surrounding land.

panicle: compound raceme or branched cluster of flowers.

pectin: any of various water-soluble colloidal carbohydrates that occur in ripe fruit and vegetables; used in making fruit jellies and jams.

pemmican: lean dried meat pounded fine and mixed with melted fat; used especially by North American Indians.

perennial: a plant lasting for three seasons or more.

perianth: outer parts of a flower enclosing the stamens and pistils.

petal: part of the perianth that is usually brightly colored.

pistil: the female ovule-bearing part of a flower.

pit: see stone.

poke: a bag.

pome: a fleshy fruit (apple or pear or related fruits) having seed chambers and an outer fleshy part.

potherb: any of various herbaceous plants whose leaves or stems or flowers are cooked and used for food or seasoning.

raceme: usually elongate cluster of flowers along the main stem in which the flowers at the base open first.

rachis: axis of a compound leaf or compound inflorescence.

receptacle: enlarged tip of a stem that bears the floral parts.

runner: see stolon.

saponins: any of various plant glucosides that form soapy lathers when mixed with water.

sepal: one of the often green parts that form the outer floral envelope or layer of the perianth enclosing and supporting the developing bud.

serrated: notched like a saw.

shrub: a low woody perennial plant usually having several major stems.

species: taxonomic group whose members can interbreed.

sphagnum: any of various pale or ashy mosses of the genus Sphagnum whose decomposed remains form peat.

spike: an indeterminate inflorescence bearing sessile flowers on an unbranched axis.

spikelet: a small sharp-pointed tip resembling a spike on a stem or leaf.

stamen: the male reproductive organ of a flower.

stigma: the apical end of the style where deposited pollen enters the pistil.

style: the narrow elongated part of the pistil between the ovary and the stigma.

stone: the hard, inner (usually woody) layer of the pericarp of some fruits (such as peaches, plums, cherries or olives) that contains the seed.

stolon: a horizontal branch from the base of a plant that produces new plants from buds at its tips.

subalpine: growing at high altitudes.

swamp: low land that is seasonally flooded; has more woody plants than a marsh and better drainage than a bog.

tepal: an undifferentiated part of a perianth that cannot be distinguished as a sepal or a petal (as in lilies and tulips).

terminal: being or situated at an end.

tendril: slender stem-like structure by which some twining plants attach themselves to an object for support.

trailing: hanging loosely along the ground.

tree: a tall perennial woody plant having a main trunk and branches forming a distinct elevated crown.

tundra: a vast treeless plain in the Arctic regions where the subsoil is permanently frozen.

umbel: flat-topped or rounded inflorescence in which the individual flower stalks arise from about the same point; youngest flowers are at the center.

vein: any of the vascular bundles or ribs that form the branching framework of conducting and supporting tissues in a leaf or other plant organ.

whorl: a round shape formed by a series of concentric circles (as formed by leaves or flower petals).

Alaback, Paul, Carol Brewer and Josh Burnham. *Northern Rockies Natural History Guide* [http://nhguide.dbs.umt.edu/] University of Montana - Missoula (2012)

Baldwin, Bruce G. *The University and Jepson Herbaria* [http://ucjeps.berkeley.edu/main/directory.html] University of California, Berkely (2012)

Becking, Rudolf W. *Pocket Flora of the Redwood Forest* (Island Press, 1982)

Beidleman, Linda H., Richard G. Beidleman and Beatrice E. Willard. *Plants of Rocky Mountain National Park* (Globe Pequot, 2000)

Benoliel, Doug and Mark Orsen. *Northwest Foraging: The Classic Guide to Edible Plants of the Pacific Northwest* (Skipstone, 2011)

Black, Merel R. and Emmet J. Judziewicz. *Wildflowers of Wisconsin and the Great Lakes Region: a Comprehensive Field Guide* (Univ of Wisconsin Press, 2009)

Brayshaw, T.C. and E.H. Garman. *Trees and Shrubs of British Columbia* (UBC Press, 1996)

Burrell, C. Colston, Janet Marinelli and Bonnie Harper-Lore. *Native Alternatives to Invasive Plants* (Brooklyn Botanic Garden, 2006)

Campbell, Paul. *Survival Skills of Native California* (Gibbs Smith, 1999)

Clemants, Steve, Steven Earl Clemants and Carol Gracie. *Wildflowers In The Field and Forest: A Field Guide to the Northeastern United States* (Oxford University Press, 2006)

Cody, William J., National Research Council of Canada. *Flora of the Yukon Territory* (NRC Research Press, 2000)

Coffin, Barbara and Lee Pfannmuller. *Minnesota's Endangered Flora and Fauna* (University of Minnesota Press, 1988)

Dawson, Elmer Yale. *The Cacti of California* (University of California Press, 1966)

Dirr, Michael A. *Dirr's Encyclopedia of Trees and Shrubs* (Timber Press, Incorporated, 2011)

Elias, Thomas S. and Peter A. Dykema. *Edible Wild Plants: a North American Field Guide* (Sterling Publishing Company, Inc., 1990)

Elias, Thomas, Thomas S. Elias and Peter A. Dykeman. *Edible Wild Plants: A North American Field Guide to Over 200 Natural Foods* (Sterling Publishing Company, Inc., 2009)

Erichsen-Brown, Charlotte. *Medicinal and Other Uses of North American Plants: A Historical Survey With Special Reference to the Eastern Indian Tribes* (Dover Publications, 1979)

Fagan, Damian. *Pacific Northwest Wildflowers: A Guide to Common Wildflowers of Washington, Oregon, Northern California, Western Idaho, Southeast Alaska, and British Columbia* (Globe Pequot, 2006)

Fernald, Merritt Lyndon, Alfred Charles Kinsey and Reed Clark Rollins. *Edible Wild Plants of Eastern North America* (Courier Dover Publications, 1958)

Fischer, Pierre C. *70 Common Cacti of the Southwest* (Western National Parks Association, 1989)

Fralish, James and Scott B. Franklin. *Taxonomy and Ecology of Woody Plants in North American Forests (Excluding Mexico and Suptropical Florida)* (John Wiley and Sons, 2002)

Freitus, Joe and Salli Haberman. *Wild Jams and Jellies Delicious Recipes Using 75 Wild Edibles* (Cambridge University Press, 2005)

Hallworth, Beryl and Chendanda Chengappa Chinnappa. *Plants of Kananaskis Country in the Rocky Mountains of Alberta* (University of Alberta, 1997)

Hickey, Michael and Clive King, *100 Families of Flowering Plants* (Cambridge University Press, 1988)

Hjalmarsson, Jan. *Montana Plant Life - Flora and Identification of Edible, Medicinal and Poisonous Plants* [http://montana.plant-life.org/] (2012)

Hultén, Eric. *Flora of Alaska and Neighboring Territories: a Manual of the Vascular Plants* (Stanford University Press, 1968)

Janick, Jules and Robert E. Paull *The Encyclopedia of Fruits and Nuts* (CABI, 2008)

Jennings, Neil L. *Coastal Beauty: Wildflowers and Flowering Shrubs of Coastal British Columbia and Vancouver Island* (Rocky Mountain Books Ltd, 2011)

Jennings, Neil L. *Central Beauty: Wildflowers and Flowering Shrubs of the Southern Interior of British Columbia* (Rocky Mountain Books Ltd, 2008)

Jennings, Neil L. *Prairie Beauty: Wildflowers of the Canadian Prairies* (Rocky Mountain Books Ltd, 2011)

Jennings, Neil L. *Uncommon Beauty: Wildflowers and Flowering Shrubs of Southern Alberta and Southeastern British Columbia* (Rocky Mountain Books Ltd, 2006)

Kelso, Fran. *Plant Lore of an Alaskan Island: Foraging in the Kodiak Archepelago* (AuthorHouse, 2011)

Kershaw, Linda. *Edible and Medicinal Plants of the Rockies* (Lone Pine Pub., 2000)

Kershaw, Linda. *Rare Vascular Plants of Alberta* (University of Alberta, 2001)

Kirkwood, Joseph Edward. *Northern Rocky Mountain Trees and Shrubs* (Stanford University Press, 1930)

Klinkenberg, Brian. (Editor) *E-Flora BC: Electronic Atlas of the Flora of British Columbia* [http://eflora.bc.ca] Lab for Advanced Spatial Analysis, Department of Geography, University of British Columbia, Vancouver (2012)

Ladd, Douglas M. *North Woods Wildflowers: A Field Guide to Wildflowers of the Northeastern United States and Southeastern Canada* (Globe Pequot, 2001)

Lahring, Heinjo. *Water and Wetland Plants of the Prairie Provinces* (CPRC Press 2003)

Larson, Lyndsey. *Central Yukon Species Inventory Project* [http://www.flora.dempstercountry.org] Friends of Dempster Country (2012)

Lesica, Peter. *A flora of Glacier National Park, Montana* (Oregon State University Press, 2002)

Li, Thomas S. C., Thomas H. J. Beveridge, *National Research Council Canada. Sea Buckthorn (Hippophae Rhamnoides L.): Production and Utilization* (NRC Research Press, 2003)

MacKinnon, Andy. *Edible & Medicinal Plants of Canada* (Lone Pine Pub., 2009)

Marsh, Chris. *Plants For A Future* [http://pfaf.org] (2012)

McKenny, Margaret and Roger Tory Peterson. *A Field Guide to Wildflowers: Northeastern and North-central North America* (Houghton Mifflin Harcourt, 1998)

McMinn, Howard. *An Illustrated Manual of California Shrubs* (University of California Press, 1951)

Moerman, Daniel E. *Native American Ethnobotany* [http://herb.umd.umich.edu/] University of Michigan - Dearborn (2012)

Moerman, Daniel E. *Native American Food Plants: An Ethnobotanical Dictionary* (Timber Press, 2010)

Mohlenbrock, Robert H. *Acanthaceae to Myricaceae: Water Willows to Wax Myrtles* (SIU Press, 2008)

Mohlenbrock, Robert H. *Flowering Plants: Pokeweeds, Four-o'clocks, Carpetweeds, Cacti, Purslanes, Goosefoots, Pigweeds, and Pinks* (SIU Press, 2001)

REFERENCES

Moss, Ezra Henry and John G. Packer. *Flora of Alberta: A Manual of Flowering Plants, Conifers, Ferns, and Fern Allies Found Growing Without Cultivation in the Province of Alberta, Canada* (University of Toronto Press, 1983)

Peterson, Lee Allen and Roger Tory Peterson. *Field Guide to Edible Wild Plants: Eastern and Central North America* (Houghton Mifflin Harcourt, 1999)

Petrides, George A. *A Field Guide to Trees and Shrubs: Northeastern and North-Central United States and Southeastern and South-Central Canada* (Houghton Mifflin Harcourt, 1973)

Petrides, George A. *Trees of the Rocky Mountains and Intermountain West* (Stackpole Books, 2005)

Phillips, H. Wayne. *Central Rocky Mountain Wildflowers: Including Yellowstone and Grand Teton National Parks* (Globe Pequot, 1999)

Phillips, Wayne. *Northern Rocky Mountain Wildflowers* (Globe Pequot, 2001)

Preston, Richard Joseph and Richard R. Braham. *North American Trees* (Iowa State Press, 2003)

Primrose, Mary and Marian Munro. *Wildflowers of Nova Scotia, New Brunswick & Prince Edward Island* (Formac Publishing Company, 2003)

Reaume, Tom. *620 Wild Plants of North America: Fully Illustrated* (CPRC Press, 2009)

Roe, E. P. *Success With Small Fruits* (Collier, 1881)

Royer, France and Richard Dickinson. *Plants of Alberta: Trees, Shrubs, Wildflowers, Ferns, Aquatic Plants, and Grasses* (Lone Pine Pub., 2007)

Royer, France and Richard Dickinson. *Wild flowers of Edmonton and Central Alberta* (University of Alberta, 1996)

Runesson, Ulf T. *Borealforest.org* [http://borealforest.org]. Faculty of Natural Resources Management, Lakehead University (2012)

Small, Ernest and Paul M. Catling, National Research Council Canada. *Canadian Medicinal Crops* (NRC Research Press, 1999)

Stuart, John David and John O. Sawyer. *Trees and Shrubs of California* (University of California Press, 2001)

Taylor, Ronald J. and George Wayne Douglas. *Mountain Plants of the Pacific Northwest: A Field Guide to Washington, Western British Columbia, and Southeastern Alaska* (Mountain Press Publishing, 1995)

Tucker, Arthur O. and Thomas DeBaggio. *The Big Book of Herbs: a Comprehensive Illustrated Reference to Herbs of Flavor and Fragrance* (Interweave Press, 2000)

Turner, Nancy J. *Food Plants of Coastal First Peoples* (UBC Press, 1995)

Turner, Nancy J. and P. Von Aderkas. *The North American Guide To Common Poisonous Plants and Mushrooms* (Timber Press, 2009)

Underhill, J. E. *Northwestern Wild Berries* (Hancock House, 1979)

US Forest Service. *Fire Effects Information System* [http://www.fs.fed.us/database/feis/] (2012)

USDA, NRCS. *The PLANTS Database* [http://plants.usda.gov, 13 July 2012] National Plant Data Team, Greensboro, NC 27401–4901 USA (2012)

Varner, Collin. *Plants of the Whistler Region* (Global Professional Publishing, 2004)

Viereck, Leslie A. and Elbert Luther Little, *Alaska Trees And Shrubs* (University of Alaska Press, 2007)

Williamson, Darcy. *The Rocky Mountain Wild Foods Cookbook.* (Caxton Press, 1995)

PHOTO CREDITS

CONTRIBUTORS

Lauren Ackein: 22b; Larry Andreasen: 22a; Aaron Arthur: 24b, 36c; Tom Ballinger: 7b, 20c; Matt Below: 40c; Bern (flickr user mythos.usa): 47b; Avis Boutell: 43b; Eileen Brown: 63b; Francesca Carmona: 46b; Allan Carson: 30b, 34a, 54c; Central Yukon Species Inventory Project: 56a, 52b, 62b; George P. Chamuris, Ph.D: 38a, 38b, 38c; Kelvin Chau: 9c, 14c; Jerritt Collord: 6a; Alfred Cook: 2b, 3b, 3c, 5a, 8b, 16b, 56c; Jim Cornish: 65b; Elisabeth Didriksen: 10a; George Dixon: 8a, 54a, 64a; Johnida Dockens: 36b; Karen Dozier: 57b; Paul S. Drobot: 52a; Anne Elliott: *vi*-a, 2c, 6b, 12a, 18a, 18b, 20b, 21b, 21c, 25a, 31a, 32a, 35a, 37a, 42a, 57a, 66b; Franco Folini: 9a, 9b; James Gaither: 24a; Theodore Garver: 4b; Herman Giethoorn: 39b, flickr.com/photos/hgiethoorn/; Matt Goff: 55a; Harry Guiremand: 32b; Emma Harrower: 48b; Dave Ingram: 11a, 55b; Walter Judd: 49b; Jozien Keijzer: 50b; Tom Kent: 19a; Linda Kershaw: 3a, 45c, 49a, 52b, 54b, 68b; Russ Kleinman: 21a, 28a, 28c; Matt Lavin: 17c, 33a, 33b, 36a, 39a, 40b, 40a, 59c, 61b, 63a, 68a; Ulrich Lorimer: 19b; Gretchen M: 37b; Esa Malila 13b; Steve Matson: 512, 53b; Joe Mckenna: 61c; Clea Moray: 29b; Alexandra Mueller: 44a, 44b; Amy O'Neill Houck: 13a; Øyvind Tafjord: 10a; Vicky Padgett: 50a; Jean Pawek: 53a; Randee Peterson: *viii*-a, 17a, 17b; Corey Raimond: 27c; Clifford A. Reiter: 29a; Christine Roberts: 58a, 58b; Réal Sarrazin: 49c; Lynette Schimming: *i*-a, 47a; Jennifer Schlick: 23b; Dr. Ahlert Schmidt: *v*-a, 5b; Dana Schwehr: 1a, 48a; Shirley Sekarajasingham: 11b; Handan Selamoglu: 28b; Jean Simard: 67a; Tania Simpson: 26a; Virginia Skilton: 7a; Robert Strusievicz: 66a; Hege Svendsen: 10d; Roland Tremblay: 65a; Dylon Whyte: 64b; Diane Williamson: *viii*-b; LaWatha Wisehar: 61a;

CREATIVE COMMONS & PUBLIC DOMAIN IMAGES

The following works are licenced under the Creative Commons or are available in the public domain. Each entry gives the photographer name followed by photo page numbers and positions. The label "own work" indicates that the photo is an unaltered work, whereas the label "deriv" indicates that the image is a derivative work, as defined by the associated Creative Commons license. The code "CC BY 2.0" refers to creativecommons.org/licenses/by/2.0/. The code "CC BY 2.5" refers to creativecommons.org/licenses/by/2.5/. The code "CC BY 3.0" refers to creativecommons.org/licenses/by/3.0/. The code "CC BY ND 2.0" refers to creativecommons.org/licenses/by-nd/2.0/. The code "PD" refers to works in the public domain.

Piero Amorati: 62a [CC BY 3.0, deriv], *via Bugwood.org*; Arild Andersen: 46a [CC BY ND 2.0, own work], *via flickr.com*; Joost J. Bakker: 42c [CC BY 2.0, deriv], *via flickr.com*; David Berger: 35b [CC BY 2.0, deriv], *via flckr.com*; Maja Dumat: 59b [CC BY 2.0, deriv], *via flickr.com*; Jacob Enos: 12b [CC BY 2.0, deriv], *via flickr.com*; Emma Forsberg: 34b [CC BY 2.0, deriv], *via flickr.com*; Marshal Hedin: 26b [CC BY 2.0, deriv], *via flickr.com*; Jessie Hey: 43a [CC BY 2.0, deriv], *via flickr.com*; Jason Hollinger: 8c, 16a, 25b, 31c, 32c, 67b [CC BY 2.0, deriv], *via flickr.com*; Opiola Jerzy: 60b, 60c [CC BY 2.5, deriv] *via Wikimedia Commons*; Jerry Kirkhart: 15a [CC BY 2.0, deriv] *via flickr.com*; Hans Kylberg: 42b [CC BY 2.0, deriv] *via flickr.com*; Leo-setä: 4a [CC BY 2.0, deriv] *via flickr.com*; Lydur Skulason: 45a [CC BY 2.0, deriv] *via flickr.com*; František Pleva: 60a [PD] *via http://www.biolib.cz*; Dave Powell, USDA Forest Service: 30a, 59a [CC BY 3.0, deriv] *via Bugwood.org*; Arnstein Rønning: 45b [CC BY 3.0, deriv] *via Wikimedia Commons*; Tero Saarni: 4c [CC BY 2.0, deriv] *via flickr.com*; Leslie Seaton: 15b [CC BY 2.0, deriv] *via flickr.com*; Walter Siegmund: 2a, 20a, 22c, 41a, 41b, 57c [CC-BY-2.5, deriv] *via Wikimedia Commons*; Peter Stevens: 18c, 41c [CC BY 2.0, deriv] *via flickr.com*; Superior National Forest: 27b, 51a [CC BY 2.0, deriv] *via flickr.com*; Nadia Talent: 44c [PD] *via Wikimedia Commons*; U.S. Geological Survey: 27a [PD] *via http://www.pwrc.usgs.gov*; Miguel Vieira: 15c [CC BY 2.0, deriv] *via flickr.com*; Liz West: 31b [CC BY 2.0, deriv] *via flickr.com*; Masayo Wright: 10b; 10c; 14a; 14b [CC BY 2.0, deriv] *via flickr.com*;

INDEX

Made in the USA
Middletown, DE
30 May 2017